MW01527471

ALL THE SHIP'S MEN

O hear us when we cry to Thee,

for those in peril on the sea.

– *Naval Hymn*

ALL THE SHIP'S MEN

HMCS *Athabaskan*'s Untold Stories

Sherry J. Pringle

Vanwell Publishing Limited
St. Catharines, Ontario

Vanwell Publishing acknowledges the financial support of the Government of Canada through the Book Publishing Development Program for our publishing activities.

Design: Linda Moroz-Irvine

Published by:
Vanwell Publishing Limited
P.O. Box 2131, 1 Northrup Crescent
St. Catharines, Ontario L2R 7S2
905 937-3100 ext. 829
905 937-1760 Fax
sales@vanwell.com
Customer Service and Orders:
1-800-661-6136

Library and Archives Canada Cataloguing in Publication
Pringle, Sherry J.
    All the ship's men : the HMCS Athabaskan's untold stories / Sherry J. Pringle.

Includes bibliographical references.
ISBN 978-1-55068-988-4

    1. Athabaskan (Ship : 1940-1944). 2. World War, 1939-1945--Naval operations, Canadian. 3. World War, 1939-1945--Personal narratives, Canadian. I. Title.

VA400.5.A84P75 2010   940.54'5971   C2010-901480-4

Front cover: "Death of a Warrior" by Sherry J. Pringle
Back cover: "HMCS *Athabaskan* on Patrol" by Sherry J. Pringle

Contents

Preface

AS THE SOUNDS OF WAR SUBSIDE and the smoke settles over the battlegrounds, the debates amongst the scholars and historians commence, to assess the successes and failures of the warring parties.

When the tally is completed and the scores on life and death have been recorded, one thing is for certain: no war is won by the latest in technology alone. Tanks, guns and mortars alone do not win wars. No, wars are won by the brains and the brawn, the blood and the sweat of the men and women involved in fighting them. The sacrifice of lives lost can never be redeemed. Effects of combat resonate past the present generation and continue to permeate the future generations of grieving families. In this story of HMCS *Athabaskan*, there are no less than one hundred and twenty-eight grieving families, who have been scarred by the ultimate sacrifice, making this Canada's largest naval disaster as a result of surface action.

Our family was one of the many affected by this tragedy. A branch is missing from our ancestral tree with the untimely death of a young uncle, Maurice Waitson.

Initially my intent was solely to learn about Moe's life and to discover how he died. However, along the way, I became acquainted with a number of his comrades and their families. Every man or woman in war has a story to tell. The *Athabaskan* story is an intriguing one.

From coast to coast in this great country of Canada, I now have numerous friends from the Athabaskan network. Some of their stories are similar to mine — extended family members who had no insight into their loved one's lives until they joined the Athabaskan Association and discovered the remaining sailors who had known them. I began my quest on the scene fifty-seven years after the tragedy. Still, some have come after me. They have come for the same reasons, looking for answers into their father, uncle, or grandfather's lives; some morsel of evidence that they did indeed exist.

The dwindling numbers of *Athabaskan* survivors are accustomed to the phone calls now. They have welcomed these intruders with open arms. When someone makes contact with one of the seamen, the news filters through the telephone lines, across the country, until someone who knew that lost soul is put in touch with the inquirer. No question is too small to ask. While any of the survivors remain, no time is ever too late to join the link.

The Athabaskans gather to pay homage to their fallen comrades every year close to the date of the disaster. At my first memorial service held on the HMCS *Haida*, we had formed a circle for the service and began singing the mournful "Naval Hymn," when one of the wives put her arms around my shoulders and whispered in my ear "You are one of us now!" We are a tightly knit group of immediate and extended family of Athabaskans.

Although the HMCS *Athabaskan*'s loss is a tragic story, the accounts derived from the individuals involved have offered great insight into their plight. Light has been shed on their rescue and the events many experienced as prisoners of war. Some of their tales are not only of survival but also of lighter moments when a chuckle could be found lurking in the darkness of their days.

For the most part, the individual tales recorded on these pages are firsthand accounts, as they have been remembered by the surviving Athabaskans, or gleaned from the pages of their war diaries. Some distant memories of long ago events, although still so vivid, do not always align with the historical facts. Other tales have been retold to me by family members. Only two personal tales were derived from such references as Canada's War Museum, or other such documentation.

The veterans and extended family members made my task of collecting stories easy. They were eager to do all they could to assist me. Our local weekly newspaper, *The Napanee Beaver*, offered up one serendipitous finding, while I was searching through the fragile archival pages of original newspapers from 1942. The huge book shifted slightly and the pages opened to reveal a large article. The title, "Napanee Woman has Reason for Pride in Family's Record" jumped out at me. It was an interview with my grandmother Waitson.

There are no earth-shattering new theories uncovered in this book. As the most important element in war is the people who fought it, such is the case of the personal accounts of the men and women telling their stories on the following pages. Guns and tanks do not enter into the equation here, only the sacrifices made by two hundred and sixty-one men onboard a ship in enemy waters.

Three important things I learned through my research and interviews; first, every sailor, be it on the eastern shore of the Atlantic, or the western, experienced life onboard ship in the same way. While browsing through a book of German warships, I couldn't help but note that the photos were similar to those of the Allied side. Photos of young sailors at work or leisure, ships in formation of a convoy, turbulent seas, ships in dry dock, they all looked the same. Second, every single veteran can recite his or her service number without a moment's hesitation. Third, (and certainly not least in importance), I discovered what a lifesaver the Red Cross Society was, literally, during the war. Every sailor taken from the ship recalled receiving their Red Cross parcels. For the most part, survival depended on the food supplies sent to them from this humanitarian organization.

When my answers had been uncovered and Moe's friends had been found, I thought my long journey was over. Then one sunny fall day I received a phone call from the navy in Halifax, inquiring about the memorial painting I had sent to France. When I commented to the caller that April 29, 2009 would mark the sixty-fifth anniversary of *Athabaskan*'s sinking, I realized there was one more thing I had to do. I must do my part to help record their stories for future generations, before they are forever lost.

A month later, on Remembrance Day, I stood at attention beside the cenotaph in my hometown where my uncle's name is carved into the stone, and contemplated the lives of our proud, but aging veterans. The men saluting the flags of the colour party, looking smart in their navy blue blazers adorned with medals, were remembering their sacrifices and those of their comrades. My determination was renewed. I couldn't help but wonder if they were able to block out their wartime nightmares or if those events played over and over again in their minds.

The annual Athabaskan Sunday was being held on April 26, 2009 at the HMCS *Haida*, now a museum attraction permanently moored in Hamilton, Ontario. I was looking forward to attending this year's ceremony and meeting up with this year's only *Athabaskan* veteran to attend, Wilfred Henrickson. I reflected on his stories while I awaited his flight to arrive from Winnipeg.

Fate had another plan for this year's special guest, however. As the memorial service proceeded to pay tribute to the fallen Athabaskans, Wilf was making his way to be reunited with them. Wilfred Henrickson passed away simultaneously as we memorialized his ship and the events of sixty-five years past. For the first time since I had embarked upon this journey, my determination faltered momentarily as I drove home alone from the service.

Although HMCS *Athabaskan* had a brief career as a warship, she did engage in numerous missions. I have only briefly accounted for them. She and her sister ship, the *Haida*, were instrumental in paving the way for the Normandy invasion, before she was sunk.

Haida went on to enjoy a long, illustrious career as Canada's number one warrior, earning her the title of "The Most Fightingest Ship in the Navy."

For the remainder of their lives, the *Athabaskan* survivors carried the torch high in honour of their fallen comrades. It is now up to the future generations to keep the stories alive.

As you turn the pages and read the accounts of these Canadian naval seamen who were preparing the way for the great Allied invasion that helped end World War II, you will have a better understanding of their sacrifices. They are two hundred and sixty-one heroes.

Acknowledgements

FOR MY BELOVED HUSBAND LARRY, whom I have dragged across the country and over the seas on my journey of discovery, and who nodded his acceptance as I began this last mission to write a book, I am eternally grateful. Thanks to my Mom, Noreen Baker, who unlocked her private memories and shared them with me. When I picked up the telephone that day to contact Herm Sulkers, little did I know he would pave the way for my quest. We became close friends and I treasured our almost daily association until the sad day he left us to be with his comrades. I am forever in his debt.

Athabaskan's wreck would never have been discovered had it not been for Wayne Abbott and his company Northern Sky Entertainment, which, supported by History Television, funded and orchestrated the search for the lost destroyer in the waters off the coast of Brittany, France. With the assistance of French marine archeologist Jacques Ouchakoff, the wreck was finally discovered in the fall of 2002.

Many thanks to: Dr. Caroline Scott who has graciously shared her documents and stories of her late husband Lieutenant Jack Scott, and tirelessly assisted me with contacts and information; Neil and Paul Sulkers, Mark and Peter Ward, Vi Connolly for her courage when facing a three and a half year separation from Bill while he served his country, who also shared their wonderful stories; Pam and John Fairchild, whose friendship and sharing hold a big place in my heart; and to the veterans of HMCS *Athabaskan*; Glen MacNeill, the late Wilf Henrickson, Harry Hurwitz, Douglas and Ingar Laurie, and Ernie Takalo. Kim Hewitt eagerly shared his dad's stories with me and Bruce Kettles graciously allowed me to use written materials attributed to his uncle Stuart Kettles. Ed and Hugh Stewart have provided me with valuable information and documents and Wayne Abbott provided important photos of the dive.

Contributors to my story have been numerous *Athabaskan* family members, writers, historians, and former naval personnel; many thanks to Gayle Buie, Debbie Cooper, Douglas Cottrell, Max Gallant, Ardel Hitchon, Nadine Howick-Giffin, Jean Fillatre, Ralph Frayne, Sarah Hayward, Anthony Holmes, Jim L'Esperance, Ralph McIlow, Simon Muzyka, Ron and Joan Reynolds, Sharon Schinke, John Ulhmann and William Vair.

Senior historian at the Directorate of History and Heritage at the Department of National Defence, Michael Whitby, provided me with valuable expert guidance. Captain E.E. Davie, OMM CD RNC (retd) has been a supportive mentor.

Across the sea in France, I owe a big debt of gratitude to Jacques Ouchakoff, and Chantal Tardif who found a home for my memorial painting of the *Athabaskan* at Fort Montbarey museum in Brest. Colonel and Madame Boisson of Brignogan-Plages graciously sought out answers to my many questions regarding the French side of my story.

Thanks to a first-class editor, Angela Dobler and publishers Ben and Simon Kooter for making this all possible. Also, thanks to my writer/neighbour Marilyn Kendall who encouraged me every step of the way and made herself accessible with her expert advice; photographers Susi Walters and Michael Murphy; my son Mark and techno genius Tina Pigden, both of whom guided me through my computer nightmares; and lastly author Larry Gray and my friend, the noted Canadian historian/writer Dr. Barry Gough, who also shared the French journey so close to our hearts.

Finally to my readers, whoever you may be, thank you for reading this personal account of a naval tragedy and the effects on the families and loved ones involved. Perhaps you will have a better understanding of the legend of this ill-fated ship, of our *Athabaskan* heroes who sacrificed their lives, and the others who graciously picked up the torch. They did indeed help make the Normandy Invasion possible.

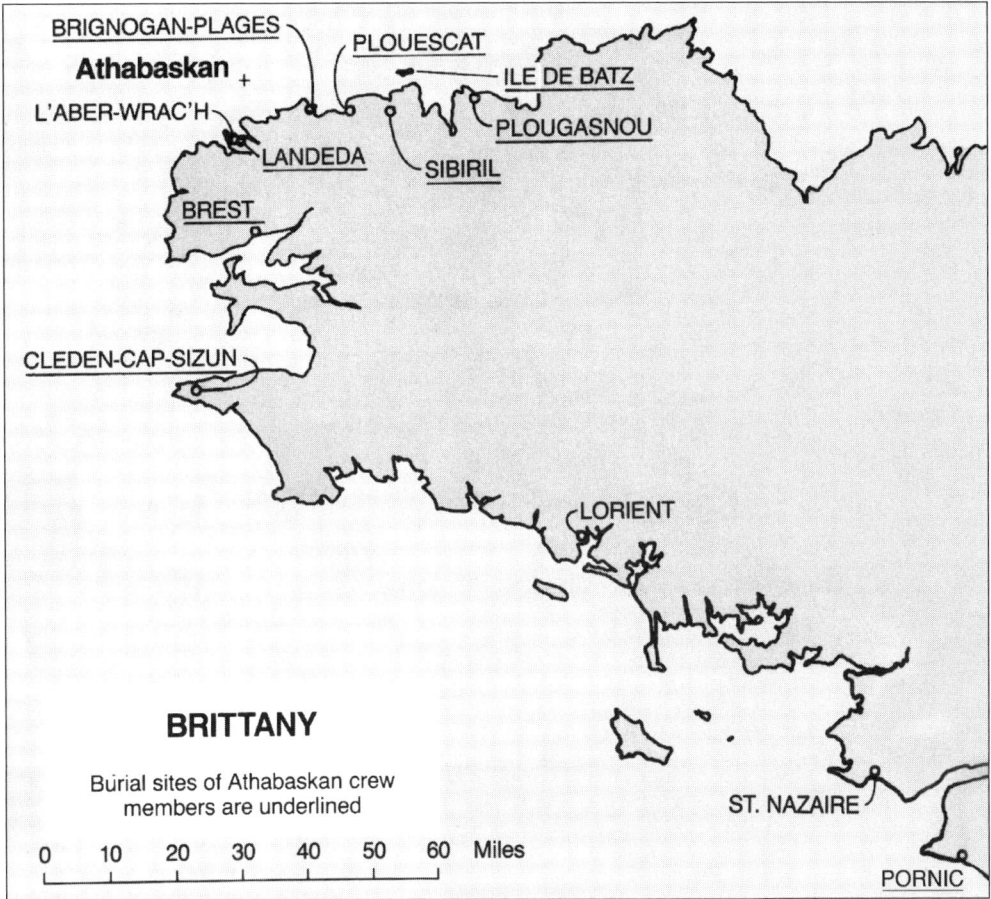

BRIGNOGAN-PLAGES

Athabaskan +

PLOUESCAT

ILE DE BATZ

L'ABER-WRAC'H

PLOUGASNOU

LANDEDA

SIBIRIL

BREST

CLEDEN-CAP-SIZUN

LORIENT

BRITTANY

Burial sites of Athabaskan crew
members are underlined

0   10   20   30   40   50   60   Miles

ST. NAZAIRE

PORNIC

This book is dedicated to Maurice Waitson AB and his fellow seamen, who lost their lives on the final mission of the HMCS *Athabaskan* on April 29, 1944, and to the survivors of that mission whose lives were forever changed by the events of history. Their courage and valour shall never be forgotten.

PART I

The Search
for Moe

NAPANEE WOMAN HAS REASON FOR PRIDE IN FAMILY'S RECORD

Six Members of Family in Navy at Present

Mrs. Stephen Waitson, Napanee, has just cause for feeling proud of the record of service which her family has given and is still continuing to give to the British and Canadian Navies.

Six of the men in her family are at present in the Navy — three brothers in the Royal Navy and three sons in the Canadian Navy. Two other brothers, who died some time ago, as a result of accidents while on active service, were also members of the Royal Navy. Besides, Mrs. Waitson's father and grandfather, who are now deceased, were also in the Royal Navy.

The record of this family would undoubtedly be difficult to duplicate in Canada. Mrs. Waitson, when interviewed by a Beaver Representative, was reluctant to have the information broadcast, but in her own quiet way indicated that she was proud of her family's record and was prevailed on to allow the story to be told.

Mr. and Mrs. Waitson have lived in Canada for some years, coming to Napanee from England, which had been their previous home. Mrs. Waitson's parents have died since the last war broke out and her 98-year-old grandmother died a short time ago, after her home had been bombed and she had spent several weeks in a bomb shelter. All the members of Mrs. Waitson's family, still living in England, have been evacuated from their original homes and it is some time since she has heard from them.

Mr. and Mrs. Waitson's three older sons, William aged 23, Stephen aged 18½ years and Maurice, 17½, are in the Royal Canadian Navy and their youngest son, who is still a young boy wants to enlist as a sea cadet. The youngest boy in the Navy, Maurice, is now on a month's leave—an especially long leave granted because of youngest son, who is still a young boy originally enlisted in the Army, but the sea was so strong in his blood that he bent every effort until he got a transfer to the Navy. The ambition of all three boys is to get into action as soon as possible and to see as much of the world as possible.

William Ford, a brother of Mrs. Waitson, who died in Napanee a few years ago, had, before coming to Canada, been a member of the Royal Navy and was for some time on the Battleship H.M.S. Queen Elizabeth. He was discharged from the Navy after falling through a hatchway, which caused an injury from which he eventually died.

Another brother, Bert, also died as a result of an accident while on active service. The other three brothers, Percy, Edward and Lancy, are still in the service.

—V—

Vegetable gardens cultivated by the

CANADA'S WAR EFFORT

A WEEKLY REVIEW OF DEVELOPMENTS ON THE HOME FRONT FROM SEPT. 24 TO OCT. 1, 1942

1. Thirteen leaders of the Communist Party of Canada, including Tim Buck of Toronto, surrender to the R.C.M.P.

2. Launching of H.M.C.C. Haida, built at famous British shipyard for Royal Canadian Navy, announced from a British port.

3. Government restricts statutory holidays to New Year's Day, Good Friday, the First Monday in July, Labor Day, Thanksgiving Day and Christmas Day, eliminating five generally observed holidays.

4. Gold mines to be asked to provide a substantial portion of the manpower required by base metal mines, Selective Service officials say in statement.

5. Elliott M. Little, Director of National Selective Service, addresses Quebec division of Canadian Manufacturers Association in Montreal.

6. Chief Justice R.A.E. Greenshields of Quebec passes away suddenly in his 82nd year.

7. Elliott M. Little, Director of National Selective Service, addresses the Canadian Chamber of Commerce at Seigniory Club.

8. New appointments affecting senior officers of the Royal Canadian Navy announced.

9. Defence Minister Hon. J. L. Ralston and Hon. C. D. Howe, Minister of Munitions and Supply, arrive in Britain by air.

10. Rev. J. S. Thomson, President of University of Saskatchewan, appointed General Manager of the Canadian Broadcasting Corporation.

11. Youths of 19 years of age and aliens within callable age groups made liable for compulsory military service in proclamation announced by War Services Minister Hon. J. T. Thorson.

12. Royal Canadian Navy ships have sunk four German U-boats and probably sunk two more in Atlantic waters during the past summer, Navy Minister Hon. Angus Macdonald announces.

—V—

Interview with Mum Waitson appeared in *Napanee Beaver*, October 7th, 1941.

Chapter One
The Premonition

AS DARKNESS FILLED THE EVENING SKIES of April 28th, 1944, it was already near-ing the dawn of a new day on the other side of the Atlantic Ocean. My grandmother "Mum Waitson" fell out of bed screaming hysterically. "Maurice is dead! The ship has sunk." My grandfather could not console her. It was late evening and they had just nice-ly gotten to sleep. She was only having a nightmare. Who wouldn't be having night-mares those days, especially Mum Waitson who had three sons in the Canadian Navy and three brothers in the Royal Navy in England. Her mother, father, siblings and nine-ty-year-old grandmother had been relocated to bomb shelters in London, England. Their neighborhood had been decimated by relentless air raid attacks. This certainly could not happen to Maurice. He was her baby. Babies didn't go to war. Why would any country allow three children from the same family to fight in a war? There was one younger child to be sure, but Maurice would always be her baby. She blamed that enlist-ing officer who permitted Moe's signature on a military document even though he knew Moe was under age. How could any man who was privy to such a lie have the courage to pass her on the street of their small town and look her straight in the eye?

Pup Waitson (Stephen was his Christian name) had immigrated to Canada in 1912. He traveled across Canada to scout out a suitable place to set up a household and await his fiancé Alma's arrival from England. After their marriage in a little white Anglican church in the village of Bath, Ontario, they moved to Hamilton, where my mother, Noreen Elizabeth was born. She was to be the eldest of their seven children. Once again Stephen and Alma moved back to the Bath area, but settling this time in Napanee. Stephen quickly settled into factory work at Gibbard Furniture, Canada's oldest estab-lished furniture manufacturer, since 1835. He was to be a craftsman there his entire working life.

Chapter Two
Growing Up Waitson

MAURICE WAS BORN MAY 5, 1924 to an already bustling household. He was the sixth child born to Alma and Stephen. One more brother, John, would complete the family. Maurice, or Moe as he was affectionately called, was only fifteen months younger than his closest brother, Stephen Jr. Stevie and he were the best of friends. They played, hunted, wrestled and were inseparable. Pup had grown up in the affluence of a large, wealthy English household. That was all gone now. He was just another ordinary working man, struggling to feed his ever growing brood. He had attended private schools, back home in London, England, where he excelled at boxing, attaining the level of golden glove.

In his new Canadian home, where everything was still strange and uncomfortable, Pup indulged his greatest skill. He coached young boxers and tested their prowess at nearby boxing competitions, sometimes as far afield as Ottawa. He was good, and his reputation preceded him everywhere he went as a boxing mentor.

Growing up in England meant that strict rules regarding behaviour were observed. The adults held the conversation, and the children were best not to be noticed. The same table manners were now observed in his own young family. Speaking at the dinner table was strictly forbidden. You learned at an early age to take what you wanted from the meat platter when it was passed, because the opportunity for a second serving was rare.

Sundays were strictly observed as days of rest. Attending Sunday school at the local Anglican Church was an essential requirement of being a young Waitson. Some Sundays, the children went to the service at the local Salvation Army in the afternoons in addition to their morning worship. Anything was better than the quiet of the day spent at home, when the children were prohibited from leaving their backyard. Although inside activities were promoted by Mum and Pup, the playing of cards was strictly forbidden.

The Great Depression had struck the world hard. Life was no different in Napanee than in larger centres. There were hard times, enough to last a lifetime.

The Waitson boys were great hunters and fishers. They spent countless hours fishing in the Napanee River behind the Gibbard Furniture factory. When the pickerel ran, they ate very well. One spring day before the legal opening of pickerel season, Moe and

Stephen were fishing at their usual haunt behind the factory. When the game warden came into view, the boys scooped up their fish and took off like a shot running for their lives. It wasn't the first time, nor would it be the last. Up and over the steep hill on the south side of the river, they ran several blocks to their large white frame house. The boys, all being very athletic, were easily able to outrun the officer. Leaving the out-of-shape warden huffing and puffing behind was no effort for the young boys. Without missing a beat, the youngsters opened the door to the woodshed behind the house, threw their fresh catch of pickerel in and continued on their escape route, through the backyards of the neighbors. The warden, now totally out of breath, began knocking on doors looking for the culprits. He eventually pounded on the Waitson door and inquired if Mum had witnessed any suspicious young lads running past her house. Bewildered at the disheveled appearance of the local warden, she said "no." The warden left in a huff to continue his interrogations of the other households. When they looked at one another with an air of curiosity, their puzzlement quickly turned to suspicion. Mum and Pup headed for the backyard where they opened the shed door, only to discover that their two sons were indeed guilty!

Summertime found the family of seven swimming at the local hangout on the river above the falls. Little bathhouses to accommodate the swimmers dotted the shores across from the historical MacPherson House in the area known as Clarksville. On hot summer days, the Waitson children would meet their friends at the water hole for lazing about, skipping stones, swimming and of course just doing kid stuff. The water there was shallow, so when the boys needed extra excitement, they would jump into the deeper water off the Centre Street bridge, located in the heart of town.

Another favourite summer pastime for the Waitson boys included spending many hours on the golf course, which was located only one block south of their house. They would scour the ditches, water hazards and rough, looking for golf balls to clean up and sell.

Winters were associated with hockey games, skating on the river and sledding down the nearby hill. Moe and Stephen were exceptional hockey players. Depression era shin pads were designed from the pages of the Eaton's Catalogue. Old catalogues could never be thrown out. They were much too valuable when the pages were wrapped tightly and tied around their legs as protection from puck hits. Former Napanee friend Tony Holmes described how they secured their depression-designer shin-pads to their legs, "We used to cut up inner tubes from old tires, into two inch strips and wrap them around the catalogues on our legs. They worked just fine until someone ran into you." When that happened, the rubber bands were cut and catalogue pages went flying helter skelter, to litter the ice surface.

At the time, there was no kids' league for hockey, only for men. Gibbards sponsored a men's league and Moe, Steve, and Tony were sequestered to play with the adults against neighboring towns. The sponsors provided the essential equipment. On one occasion an opponent picked a fight with young Tony. Out of the corner of his eye, Tony caught sight of Moe and Steve, pelting away at two members of the opposition up against the boards.

Having an in-house boxing expert had its benefits. Being well coached by their father, the two boys were more than capable of holding their own in skirmishes. Tony laughed when he recalled, "Yes, the Waitson boys were great friends. You really wanted to have them on your side."

Saturday nights were given to listening to "Amos and Andy" on the parlour's crackling radio. Of course, no radio listening was complete without popcorn. The kids anxiously awaited the designated hour for their weekly entertainment. Sometimes in the evenings they would crack open hickory nuts with a hammer so Mum could make them their favourite maple fudge.

Although times were tough, the children, raised under strict Victorian rule, still managed to have their fun. Pranks were the most wonderful outlet of all. The key to their shenanigans, like in all households full of children, was not to get caught. Sometimes it was just hard to keep the giggles and arm wrestling tiffs from giving you away.

The girls were the best part of being in a large family; there was always someone to tease or coax into a quarrel. All you had to do was pull their hair, throw out the occasional insult or simply laugh at them, and another quarrel had just begun.

Moe is remembered by his eldest sister, Noreen, as being a kind, gentle sort but he definitely had the stubborn Waitson streak. She recalled one occasion, when it was Moe's turn to purchase the meat from the local butcher shop for that night's dinner. He kicked up an awful fuss. Mum insisted it was his turn. He repeatedly refused, saying he wasn't going to walk to the shop. His friends were waiting for him at the corner and he was in a hurry to catch up with them. Mum thrust the money in his hand and sternly gave him his marching orders. He slammed the door as he left the house with the money tightly wrapped in his fist. He had no intention of obeying. Once outside the house, he laid the money down in the middle of the road, placed a small rock on top and quickly left to meet his buddies. When Moe had his mind made up there was nothing stopping him.

Chapter Three
Off to War

MOE'S OLDEST BROTHER BILL was the first to sign up for war. He joined the Canadian Navy. The Saturday cinemas in Napanee and across the country bombarded their audiences with war bond ads. Amid flying popcorn boxes and catcalls, the youth enjoyed their Saturday flicks for a nickel. The big screen made signing up to serve your country look very inviting. As the newsreels showed pictures of the new recruits carrying their duffle bags to the train station and saying farewell to their sweethearts, it evoked such a romantic feeling. Escaping this little hick town and visiting places you had only read about in the history books wasn't such a bad idea. Besides being treated like a man, you would be given three square meals a day and handed a paycheck in return for your day's work. That seemed so inviting, coming on the heels of the Depression. Yes, one had to admit, it all looked pretty appealing. There would be no more childhood restrictions to obey.

With Bill already enlisted, Moe couldn't wait to take the leap. On January 15 1942, he finally enlisted in the Canadian Navy. He was just seventeen years old! The old screen door to the sun porch squeaked as he crept out the back way and walked across town to the recruiting office. Looking disheveled from the sleepless night he'd just spent struggling with his own determination and with the knowledge he was about to disobey his parents, he walked into the recruiting station. With sweaty palms and shaky hands, he signed his name on the dotted line.

The recruiting officer knew the Waitson family well. Although he was aware that Moe was under age, he knew the war effort needed young men desperately. The Royal Navy in England had already suffered such heavy losses, that they were looking to the Canadians to reinforce their troops and fund the building of more state-of-the-art ships. The newer ships would come equipped with the latest in technology and guns and the ability to travel at higher speeds. Extra manpower was absolutely essential in order to win this war.

Stevie was the only one in whom Moe had confided, the only one who knew he was serious about enlisting. Moe threatened to box his ears if he told, but he knew Stevie would not squeal on him. Moe knew he had the same intentions but was a little more hesitant to cross Mum and Pup. Once Stevie saw what Moe had done however, he would soon follow suit.

Moe on leave in London, circa 1943.

Moe would have to face the family at the dinner table that night. Mum and Pup would be cross for a while but eventually they would see they couldn't stop his determination. They could not stay mad at him forever. Besides, when they saw him in his new uniform they would be so proud of him. In time, he knew the family would adjust to the idea of his going off to war. There was no choice here, they simply had to get used to the idea.

A couple of weeks later, it was time for Moe to leave Napanee for what would be his final time. Pup turned away so he wouldn't see the tears in his eyes. Amid the tears and bear hugs, Moe said goodbye to his family. He'd miss Mum and her famous apple pies, but he would miss Stevie and Noreen the most. Johnny was just a little boy, but he would miss teasing him. They all cried, pleaded and insisted he was too young to go to war. It just fell on deaf ears. That old door made the most deafening sound it had ever made, when he slammed it for the very last time.

He had one more task to do, which was to swing by the Mellows and say good-bye to his buddy Ralph. The hunting would have to be placed on hold for a while. Everyone said it would not be long and the world would return to its usual state, and everyone could go back to living as they did before the war. But for now, he had a mission to accomplish. Moe left his innocence and his childhood friends behind. Tony eventually joined the navy and was to serve on a corvette doing convoy duty, and Ralph joined the air force. They were never to see Moe again.

Moe's initial training at HMCS *Cataraqui* lasted almost two months, from the middle of January to March 3, 1942. He is recorded to have spent brief periods of time on HMCS *York*, *Stadacona*, *Cornwallis*, and back again to *Stadacona* until December 11, 1942.

Niobe in Scotland was his last stop for onshore training. On February 4, 1943, Moe reported for his final posting on board HMCS *Athabaskan*. He was assigned to the crew of "B" guns. There were two gun stations on *Athabaskan's* bow, one behind the other. The "A" guns were the most forward on the deck, in close proximity to the bow. The "B" gun station was on a platform above and behind the "A" position. There was a similar configuration for the two gun stations at the stern of the ship where "X" guns were mounted on a platform above "Y" guns, which were the furthest aft on the ship.

Athabaskan's deck looking forward from bridge. (courtesy Ed Stewart)

Chapter Four
Birth of a Warrior

CANADA HAD COMMISSIONED THE BRITISH to build four Tribal Class destroyers outfitted with the most current technologies. The four Tribals were named HMCS *Huron*, HMCS *Athabaskan*, HMCS *Haida*, and HMCS *Iroquois,* after native Canadian tribes. The identical ships were 377 feet long, 37 ½ feet wide, with a displacement of 3000 tons. They could attain speeds upward of 36 knots. These shining new fighting machines came with the hefty price tag of two million dollars each. Ammunition in the form of torpedoes, pom poms, star shells, Oerlikons and depth charges completed the munitions inventory. The ships were to become the pathfinders for the Normandy invasion.

Every Canadian sailor's adrenaline levels pumped sky high at the very thought of having the privilege to serve onboard a Tribal. With so much talk about the British ship *Hood* and the German *Bismarck*, Canada was about to take its place centre stage in the war arena on the high seas.

It has always been a superstition, not to be taken lightly, that a ship cannot change its name. The navy had planned to have HMCS *Iroquois* launched first. Their advertising and promotional materials all suggested that was the case. However, the *Iroquois* was heavily damaged during an air raid in the English shipyard at Newcastle-on-Tyne, where the ships were being built. The raid took place in April of 1941. It was decided by the navy to rename the *Athabaskan*, also nearing completion, the *Iroquois* and maintain

HMCS *Athabaskan* wearing camoflauge. (courtesy Ed Stewart)

her scheduled launch date. Thus, the damaged *Iroquois* became the *Athabaskan* and would be launched at a later date.

On the cloudy, cool day of November 18th, 1941, Lady Tweedsmuir, widow of Canada's first wartime Governor-General, broke a bottle of champagne over the bow of HMCS *Athabaskan*. The new ship slipped into the cold water of the River Tyne and was towed off to be outfitted for war. Thus, a warrior was born. This new warrior, conceived on British soil, and birthed into the chilly North Atlantic waters, was christened by an English aristocrat. She was never to be acquainted with her Canadian homeland.

The actual commissioning ceremony took place on February 3, 1943. Moe was stationed at *Niobe* when his call finally came on February 4th to report for detail on the *Athabaskan*. His dreams had been realized at last. Imagine what his family and friends back home in Napanee would say when they heard their small town boy was now a sailor on this fearsome new force.

Another member of the crew made its first debut aboard the ship on commissioning day. A ginger-coloured cat marched up the gangplank like it belonged there. The men quickly adopted "Ginger" as their new mascot. She was to accompany the ship and crew on all their missions, including their final voyage.

"We Fight As One" — Emblem designed by Signalman William Stewart. (Courtesy of Ed Stewart)

Chapter Five
"We Fight as One"

NEW RECRUITS BEGAN TRICKLING IN from their training stations and other assignments in various parts of Canada and the British Isles. The Canadian sailors represented every province from coast to coast. From the complement of two hundred and fifty men, there were a few seasoned sailors and the remainder were young, energetic new sailors, fresh from their months of training and eager to rise to the demands of war. As the men made themselves familiar with their new home and comrades, stores were loaded on board, making ready for her first voyage. The excitement was palpable as they prepared themselves for this highly anticipated moment. They had won the most sought after positions in the navy, and now here they were aboard the ship in the midst of the world's attention. Canada was finally a force to be reckoned with. The newly assigned ship's company now had to prepare this huge steel and rivet machine for life at sea and determine if she was capable of doing all that was expected of her.

All the preparation that had been drilled into them at training was now a fact of life. Their commander was George R. Miles. He demanded the best. Being a Canadian boy from New Brunswick, Miles was trained in Halifax and at the Royal Military College in Kingston and had spent time in the Royal Navy in England, which was a common practice of the time.

Before she could take her place on the high seas, *Athabaskan* had to prove herself seaworthy. Every moving part of the ship, be it mechanical or electrical, had to be tested. Thus followed long days of sea trials. With the ever-present threat of fires that could erupt from an enemy hit, the massive explosives or the thousands of gallons of oil onboard, fire drills were first on the agenda to be exercised.

In the exhausting days of the trials that followed, her compass was swung and everything imaginable was tested; anchors, throttles, gears, pumps and everything electrical. The ship's speed and maneuvering skills were tested and all the guns were fired in her staged dress rehearsal. After minor adjustments and alterations, the massive warrior was ready for war.

Amidst the energetic shouts of approval from onlookers, the *Athabaskan* slipped her lines at the naval dockyard and headed down the River Tyne. Captain Miles signed the official papers accepting her into the fleet of the Royal Canadian Navy. With their chests bursting with pride and excitement the ship's crew were finally on their way to their first

Damage from Glider Bomb (courtesy of Ed Stewart)

mission at Scapa Flow, with the Royal Air Force providing a fighter escort as far as Scotland.

HMCS *Athabaskan* was to have a very short career of only fifteen months, soon living up to the superstition surrounding her name change. There was no shortage of scrapes and incidents that would leave her damaged. Dry dock became her familiar second home.

On her first mission to patrol the Icelandic waters surrounding Faeroes Passage for blockade runners, she suffered hull damage due to the extreme weather conditions. Repairs in dry dock took her out of commission for five weeks.

In June of 1943, just a few months after her entry into the war, she collided with a cable at the mouth of the port at Scapa Flow, off the coast of Northern Scotland. That took another month for repairs.

During her missions of July and August of 1943, the *Athabaskan* was based in Plymouth while carrying out antisubmarine patrols in the Bay of Biscay. There she was struck by a German glider bomb (nicknamed "Chase Me Charlie"). The bombs were controlled by radio and dropped from an aircraft. They had wings like a plane, weighed in at 650 pounds and traveled at a speed of 375 miles per hour. Usually dropped right overhead, this bomb was deployed while parallel to the ship at a distance of two miles. It passed from the port side between "B" gun and the wheelhouse, through the ship and exploded twenty-five feet further on. The Germans had miscalculated the beam of the ship. Minutes later, a glider bomb struck the British ship *Egret* which was traveling

Pride of the German fleet, Scharnhorst.

Scharnhorst. (courtesy of Ed Stewart)

Moe, in foreground with gun crew, astride left gun.

Last known photo of *Athabaskan*'s company. (courtesy Ed Stewart)

as part of the same flotilla. The *Egret* sank in just fourteen seconds, taking with her two hundred sailors and leaving only thirty-five survivors.

The *Athabaskan* suffered extensive damage in this attack. Five seamen were killed, and all were buried at sea. Twelve sailors were wounded. Holes in the damaged hull were stuffed with rags, hammocks and anything the sailors could find. Captain Miles refused assistance, so it took the mighty but injured ship three days to limp all alone back to port. Only when the extensively damaged destroyer passed through the markers and into Plymouth Sound, did he grant permission, allowing it to be towed. This damage led to three months of repair in Devonport.

Christmas of 1943 found the ship again at Scapa Flow. On December 26th *Athabaskan* was providing convoy escort for a homeward bound convoy, when the Captain received word that the German battleship *Scharnhorst* had been spotted a good distance off. As the crew anxiously waited for their call to action, orders for *Athabaskan* to break away and engage in the hunt never came. Captain Stubbs kept his crew abreast of the details of *Scharnhort's* pursuit all day until the German giant was destroyed by Allied torpedoes at 1945 hours.

Conditions on board were a far cry from comfortable. The cold crept into the very bones of the crew. Gale force winds were a common occurrence in the North Sea with waves reaching the staggering height of forty feet, crashing over the decks and making it difficult to maintain one's foothold on the steel surface.

On January 8, 1944, *Athabaskan* put to sea on a secret mission with the British Ashanti and three other HMS destroyers and the battleship King George V. Rumours were flying about as to their destination and purpose. *Ashanti* and *Athabaskan* broke away from the flotilla and steamed into port in the Azores, while the remainder of the ships proceeded to Gibraltar. In the Azores, a number of *Athabaskan*'s crew went ashore for a little free time. After refueling, *Athabaskan* and *Ashanti* rendezvoused with the returning flotilla and together they proceeded home, still unaware of the importance of their escort. It was not until they returned to England on the 18th that they learned the distinguished guest they had been escorting was none other than the Prime Minister. Winston Churchill sent a message of "Well done" to the destroyers.

After the Scapa Flow mission, *Athabaskan* was assigned to the 10th Flotilla. This consisted of Canada's four Tribals, Britain's four Tribals (*Tartar*, the lead, *Eskimo*, *Ashanti*, and *Nubian*), as well as the lighter ship called *Javelin*. The rest of the ships that comprised the 10th were two Polish ships and the cruisers *Black Prince* and *Bellona*.

Once they were in stationed in England's southern port of Plymouth, rumours started circulating the ship that their Commander, George Miles, was being reassigned to another venue. Thirty-one-year-old Lieutenant-Commander John H. Stubbs from British Columbia was to be the new commander. Stubbs had come up the ranks quickly with a distinguished naval record. It did not take him long to win the admiration of his new crew.

As part of the 10th Flotilla, their offensive task was to clear the English Channel of enemy ships in preparation for the D-Day landing. Due to enemy aircraft surveillance, the Tenth

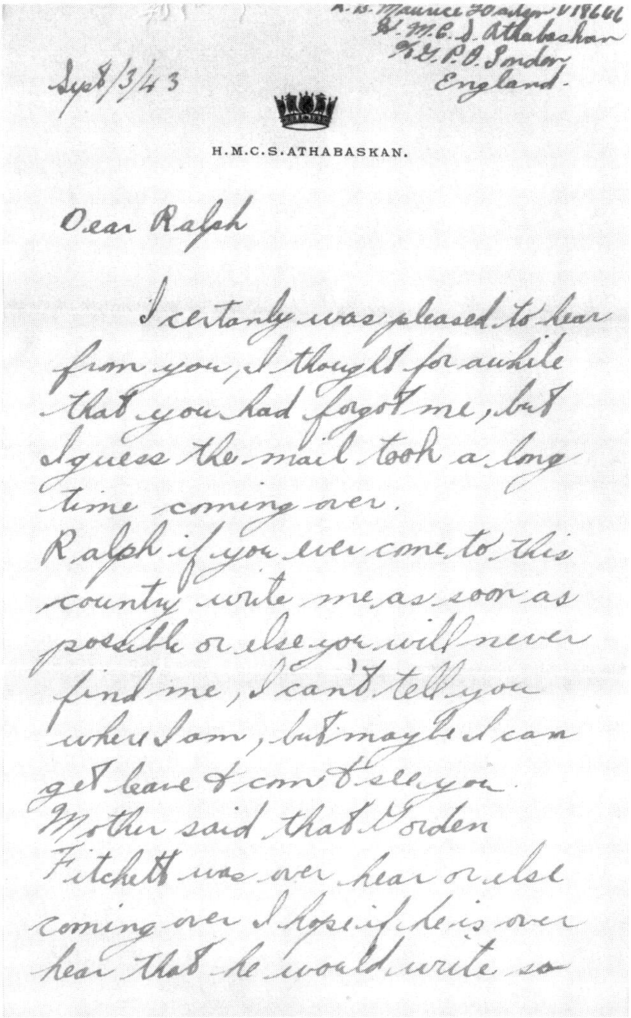

A. B. Maurice Hoalen V18646
H.M.C.S Athabaskan
G.P.O. London
England.

Sept/3/43

♔

H.M.C.S. ATHABASKAN.

Dear Ralph

I certainly was pleased to hear
from you, I thought for awhile
that you had forgot me, but
I guess the mail took a long
time coming over.
Ralph if you ever come to this
county write me as soon as
possible or else you will never
find me, I can't tell you
where I am, but maybe I can
get leave & come & see you.
Mother said that Gorden
Fitchett was over hear or else
coming over I hope if he is over
hear that he would write so

Ralph Mellow
Napanee Ont
Canada

From H. M. C. SHIP
PASSED
BY CENSOR
Signature

Flotilla Channel sweeps were done off the coast of France at night at speeds exceeding 30 knots, with radar silence. Lieutenant Jack Scott, in charge of gunnery aboard the ship, was quoted as saying:

"Early in 1944, the Tribals assumed their attack role in the English Channel. Our objective was to seek out and destroy enemy surface forces that could interfere with the invasion fleet, and possibly upset the whole invasion…The Athabaskan was a proud ship, a happy ship, and above all, an efficient ship. As a member of the crack Tenth Destroyer Flotilla, comprised of Royal Navy and Royal Canadian Tribals, she had a top reputation for efficiency and getting things done."

On the night of April 26th, 1944, while cruising the Channel, the flotilla came upon three German Elbing Class destroyers, *T24, T27* and *T29*. The formation had slightly altered course away from the gunfire seen coming from the shore batteries, when the Elbings were spotted on the radar screen.

As the 10th picked up speed to investigate, *Haida* and *Athabaskan* were in the lead, with *Huron* and *Ashanti* in formation behind. The German destroyers were traveling east under the protection of smokescreen.

Athabaskan and *Haida* gave chase to the Elbings. One ship was seen coming out of the smoke screen and then doubling back in. The two Tribals continued in their pursuit. Amidst thundering explosions of fire from all the guns blazing, they pounded the German destroyer relentlessly until geysers of sizzling steam erupted from the boilers, and flames engulfed the wounded vessel from stem to stern. *Athabaskan* and *Haida* closed in for the kill. While *T29*'s guns were still firing, her survivors were seen clamoring into life rafts. A salvo meant to strike below *T29*'s waterline slammed into her hull instead, throwing the sailors skyward. The damage was too deep and fatal for *T29* to recover. She slipped beneath the surface of the sea off the coast of Brittany, France. The time was 4:20 a.m.

Lt.Cdr. William Sclater was onboard *Haida* during the altercation the night of April 26th. He reported: "We are watching an enemy destroyer sinking. For more than a half-hour she has been a blazing wreck but until a few moments ago, [*T29*'s] guns still were spitting defiance… 'There she goes!' someone shouts and, as we watch, the blazing mass tilts over and slides under the sea. It is dark again under the stars."

The air was heavy with the smell of cordite and smoke. Shore batteries along the coast fired at the Tribals until the sky went dark again after the fire was extinguished by the sea.

According to Sclater, "It [was] time to go." After almost two hours of heavy fighting, the men could still raise 'a cheer.' Besides the one Elbing destroyer sunk by the 10th Flotilla, three other enemy ships were damaged.

Upon the Tribals' return to Plymouth Sound, sailing past all the ships at anchor there, sailors on decks saluted from both starboard and port sides. The warriors proudly flew their white ensign flags, which denoted that battle had taken place. They were the victors! Whistles, catcalls, and resounding cheers echoed throughout the Sound, welcoming home the heroes of the day.

A.B. M Watson V18644
H.M.C.S. Athabaskan
% I P.O. London
England

april 23/44

Dear Sis.

Well here I am again. I rec. your Easter card yesterday & it was darn good of you to remember me, for Easter. I guess you & Mum are the only ones that haven't forgot all about me.

How is Cec & the kids, fine I hope & also yourself. I hear Elaine is getting to be quite the girl to talk. Oh well she wouldn't be a girl if she didn't talk.

How is Paul is he still as big a devil as ever. Mum said he goes to Lunda

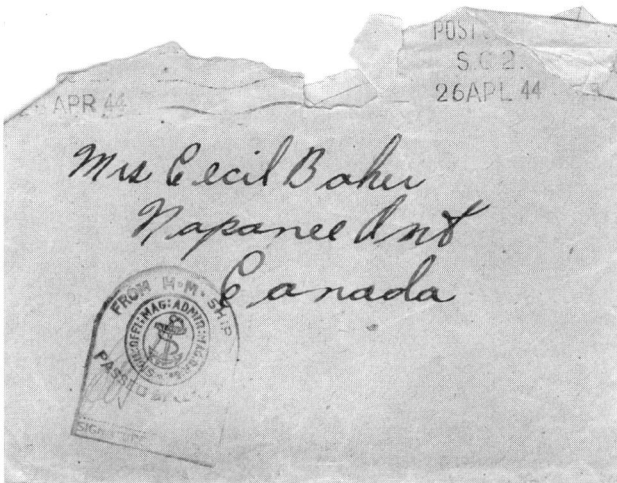

POST
S.C.2.
26 APR 44
APR 44

Mrs Cecil Baker
Napanee Ont
Canada

FROM H.M. SHIP
PASSED

Mae West Life Jacket. (courtesy Ed Stewart)

Chapter Six

Death of a Warrior

"Do not go gentle into that good night."

— Dylan Thomas

MOE'S LAST LETTER HOME to his sister Noreen was dated April 23, 1944. He talked about how quiet the sea was, so calm and eerie. He noted "the sea was like glass."

In another letter to his childhood friend Ralph Mellow in Napanee, his homesickness could be read between the lines. His friends had all been scattered to the wind with their enlistments. They had signed on to all three military branches and quickly lost touch with one another. In the letter Moe reminisced about hunting and shooting tin cans, as if longing for the good old days. He was anxious to meet up with Ralph in London the next time he was granted a few days' leave. Ralph was with the air force and did not receive the letter until he had returned home to Napanee, by which time Moe's ship had already been sunk.

The crew of the *Athabaskan* were enjoying leisure time after their harrowing ordeal of a couple of nights prior when they were chasing the enemy in the Channel. They had been under even more pressure the last few days, when they had been called upon night after night to venture into the Channel, returning at daybreak, cleaning up, reorganizing and setting out to sea again on yet another patrol. Being in Plymouth was much more enjoyable than up north, especially Scapa Flow or the Arctic, where there was nothing to do but play cards. Here in the south, they could go ashore, enjoy ale at the local pubs and let their hair down by joining in the merriment for which the British are noted.

The brotherhood between the Haidans, Athabaskans and other Tribal crews was the envy of the other warships. The men were so far from home but at least they had one another. They frequently passed time on one another's ships, wrote letters to loved ones back home and recounted the more carefree days of their youth.

In the late afternoon of April 28, 1944, the men were relaxing. Some were on shore, others were aboard *Haida*, visiting and playing cards. Those on shore in the movie house watching "Wake Island," saw a message flash over the big screen telling them to return to their ships and prepare for yet another Channel run. Their duty that night was to escort the minelayers in the waters off the coast of France.

As the *Athabaskan* slipped her mooring from the buoy affectionately known as "Canada House," their cat Ginger leapt across to the *Haida*. "This is not a good sign!" noted the men. The Haidans gently tossed her back to her home ship. There is a superstition that cats will abandon a home where death is imminent, thus the sailors' concern. As the ships pulled apart, Ginger tried to make one last attempt to jump. She was perched on the gunwale of the boat with her claws digging in, ready to spring in one last-ditch effort. Someone quickly grabbed her in the nick of time. The crew of both ships now had an uneasy feeling that a bad omen had taken up residence over their heads like a big black cloud.

The seas were calm with a low swell as they slid from port and entered the Sound. The sky was clear and the moon was shining over the procession below. This was going to be yet another sleepless night. The strain of the previously fought battle was still vivid in their minds. As the entourage headed for France's unfriendly shores, the sailors were much more solemn than usual.

The 10th Flotilla was traveling with only half its offensive power. *Huron* and *Ashanti* had had a minor collision while on mission on the 26th and were both out of commission. *Tartar* was also out for refit. Therefore, the two destroyers, *Haida* and *Athabaskan* were the only support force that night. It was the only time they had been sent out alone.

The minelayers on this particular night had left port earlier to get a head start on their mission. The time was 2000 hours. It was the last time the sister ships would ever be together in port. At 0200 hours, Plymouth signaled the vessels that two enemy ships were in their vicinity. The ships turned out to be *T24* and *T27*, which they had encountered on the evening of April 26th. They were ghosting the shore, making their way to the port city of Brest for repairs.

Orders were issued to give chase. Gunfire erupted from the 10th Flotilla, with *Haida* and *Athabaskan* both firing their guns. *Haida* was using newly issued flashless cordite for the first time that night. Since the Germans couldn't see her gunfire, they turned their attention to the *Athabaskan*.

At 4:17 a.m. *Athabaskan* was rocked by a tremendous explosion as a torpedo struck her stern portside, knocking out "X" and "Y" gun stations. The ship's propellers stopped. *Athabaskan* lay wounded and vulnerable in the water. Captain Stubbs radioed *Haida* to report her condition and the reply returned was to prepare to be towed. "Y" gun crew had been decimated immediately, with one lone survivor. Moe had just been assigned duty on "X" guns on the first of April and was therefore in the midst of the chaos.

"B" guns were still firing fast and furiously from their mount on the forward deck while some crewmembers were trying valiantly to put out the fires that had erupted, when Captain Stubbs gave the command, "Prepare to abandon ship." The sailors made their way to their designated stations. Approximately ten minutes after the first torpedo struck, a second thunderous explosion ripped the stern from the ship. This second catastrophic assault occurred in the hull just abaft the break in the focs'le on the starboard side.

Hell and damnation could not have unleashed a more fearsome display of fury than the fire and destruction that was hurtled into the cool April night sky. With a terrible roar, intense heat and flames leapt high into the heavens. Black billowing smoke from the burning oil and chunks of shredded steel, pipes, and gratings from the giant warship flew through the air as if they were mere toys being tossed about effortlessly. Smoke was sucking oxygen from the atmosphere making it almost impossible to breathe. Scalding steam was spewing into the air like an angry volcano eruption. A raging inferno of fire and flames engulfed everything from the No.1 boiler to the stern of the ship. Earth shattering explosions from the ammunition supplies pierced the sky in every direction. The men tried hard to protect their faces from the intense heat, which caused severe burns to their faces and hands. The sleek grey fighting machine had been reduced to a giant blazing blowtorch.

Haida quickly laid a smokescreen over *Athabaskan* for temporary protection from the enemy and then turned her attention to giving chase to the two Elbings. She managed to barrage *T27* with incessant gunfire and chased her with a hateful vengeance until the German destroyer ran hard aground onto Brittany's rocky coast. The enemy's decks immediately lit up with the eruption of fires and the sound of explosions could be heard miles out to sea.

Meanwhile, Captain Stubbs gave his final order to "Abandon Ship!" There was no panic, Captain Stubbs appeared calm and in control. Crewmembers helped their injured comrades over the sides of the ship before jumping themselves. For the men below decks, the orders were shouted down through the port hatches to get out immediately. Athabaskans jumped or were blasted into the frigid waters of the North Atlantic. From the intense heat of the fires and hot steam, the men leapt into the cold Channel waters, estimated to be 55 degrees Fahrenheit, now red with burning oil.

Oil and fire were everywhere. The billowing smoke from the explosions could be seen by the returning minelayers thirty miles to the north. Athabaskan fought back hard, but the damage she sustained was too extensive. It was destined to be her last battle. The mighty destroyer pointed her bow skyward as if offering one final salute to the heavens and gave up her fight. She slipped quietly beneath the surface into the dark waters of the Channel.

Sailors swam through raging fires of burning oil, bumping into their dead or unconscious comrades. With their bodies badly burned and faces covered in oil, they were beyond recognition.

Haida returned to rescue what remained of the *Athabaskan* crew, lighting up the predawn sky with starshell so as not to collide with its debris. At first the Haidans did not see any sign of the disaster. However, through the earphones of the anti-submarine sonar could be heard the splashing in the water created by the sailors thrashing about. Shortly thereafter, the Haidans could smell the sickening scent of oil. As the oil lay covering the sea, hundreds of little yellow lights glowing on the dark surface were seen twinkling about everywhere, bobbing like corks on the crest of the sea. All the men were wearing newly issued Mae West life jackets with crotch straps to prevent them from drowning. As part of their issue, little lights adorned the top of each hood, acting as a tiny beacon. When the men pulled on the chinstraps the little lights were activated.

All was silent as *Haida* plied the waters searching for survivors. Occasionally someone yelled "Over here!" Debris and bodies were everywhere. Nothing was recognizable. The ship had simply vanished from the surface. War had just taken on a new reality. It had finally claimed one of the Tribals. What was left of a fierce and mighty warrior was now just a pile of floating rubble.

Back in England, Central Command ordered *Haida* to return to port, fearing retaliation by enemy air strikes now that the night sky was giving way to dawn. They were in an increasingly vulnerable position with the impending daybreak. *Haida*'s commander ordered everything possible to be lowered into the water to assist in the rescue of *Athabaskan*'s crew, including their carley floats, cork nets, the whaler and motor cutter. Commander DeWolf started a countdown, "five minutes, four minutes..." He could stay no longer for the rescue without placing his own vessel in jeopardy.

Three Haidans stayed behind in the motor cutter to pick up survivors. They had six onboard along with a couple of their own men who had been left on the cork nets when the captain ordered the engines slow ahead.

One can only imagine the agony Captain DeWolf endured over obeying Central Command. They had been sister ships. The Athabaskans were one with their comrades on *Haida*. They were countrymen who had served on missions together, shared the same training, and saluted the same flag. How could he possibly leave all these men to succumb to the freezing waters? What would become of them? In the end, orders had to be obeyed; DeWolf, knowing he was precariously close to a German minefield, reluctantly gave the command to swing the ship north and head for port in England. As the ship picked up speed and the waters became more turbulent with the wake, *Haida* left the tragic scene behind. Attempts to rescue *Athabaskan*'s survivors had lasted only eighteen minutes. God have mercy on them all!

DeWolf radioed C-in-C in Plymouth and declared: "One Elbing Class destroyer hit and driven ashore in flames near Isle de Vierge. One Elbing Class destroyer damaged, escaped to eastward. *Athabaskan* torpedoed and sunk. Have picked up survivors and am returning to harbour. Request fighter protection. *Haida*."

Meanwhile, Central Command had ordered British MTBs, which had been part of their hostile operation, to rush to the scene to pick up survivors. At 5:37 a.m., thinking they would be unable to arrive before daybreak, the orders were canceled. DeWolf had left the scene of the tragedy believing help was on its way.

Haida returned home alone, with her fighting partner gone. On previous missions when they flew their battle ensign, it was with pride. This time, their white ensign flapped all alone in the sky from its yardarm. This brave warship was met by two British destroyers, HMS *Offa* and HMS *Orwell*, which escorted her to port. As they entered the sound this time, their welcome home was much more subdued as rumours of *Athabaskan*'s demise, traveling like wildfire, had quickly spread to the other ships.

Meanwhile, *Haida*'s cutter with its survivors was also homeward-bound. However, the boat's motor was temperamental and had to be restarted several times. The Germans chased them but gave up as the cutter drifted into the vicinity of a minefield.

HMCS *Athabaskan*'s brief, fifteen-month career as a warrior had been painted with a black brush from the very beginning. She was the original HMCS *Iroquois*, damaged in the shipyard, with her name now changed to *Athabaskan*. By the time her fight was over, she had endured stress damage, a collision, an attack by a glider bomb and finally total destruction, all in a very short period of time.

"X" Gun Crew. (courtesy Ed Stewart)

"Death of a Warrior" Inspired by Herm Sulkers, Painted by Sherry Pringle

Department of National Defence
Naval Service

Ottawa, Canada

1 May, 1944.

Dear Mrs. Waitson:

It is with deepest regret that I must confirm the telegram of the 1st of May, 1944, from the Minister of National Defence for Naval Services, informing you that your son, Maurice Waitson, Able Seaman, Royal Canadian Naval Volunteer Reserve, Official Number V-18646, is missing from H.M.C.S. "Athabaskan".

According to the report received from overseas, your son's loss occurred when H.M.C.S. "Athabaskan" was torpedoed and sunk by enemy action on the 29th of April, 1944, in the English Channel. Further particulars of this Naval disaster are being published in the newspapers.

While Able Seaman Waitson is reported as "missing", there is a possibility of his survival. It is understood that a number of the crew have been taken prisoners of war by the enemy. The Red Cross have been informed and are attempting to obtain from the German Government a list of those taken. Please be assured that as soon as any further information respecting your son has been received you will be informed.

Please allow me to express the sincere sympathy of the Minister of National Defence for Naval Services, the Chief of the Naval Staff and the Officers and men of the Royal Canadian Navy, the high traditions of which your son has helped to maintain.

Yours sincerely,

SECRETARY, NAVAL BOARD.

Mrs. Alma Waitson,
Napanee, Ontario.

H.Q. 11
35M—10-42 (6522)
H.Q. 814-16-1

The dreaded letter. (courtesy of the author)

Chapter Seven
The Aftermath

WHAT HAPPENED TO MOE? Had he survived the carnage? Did he manage to be rescued by the enemy? The mighty warship had set sail on a clear night and never returned home. Of her crew of two hundred and sixty-one, one hundred and twenty-eight young Canadian men perished, along with their mascot Ginger. No less than one hundred and fifteen of the casualties were under the age of thirty. Husbands, fathers, sons and brothers were gone forever. Innocence died on that day of April 29, 1944.

The Haidans had great difficulty rescuing the Athabaskan sailors from their rope ladders and pulling them safely onboard their ship. The men would grab a sailor by the arms, pants, anything they could get hold of, only to have a number of them slip out of their grasp, because they were so covered in oil.

Captain Stubbs helped Teddy Hewitt up *Haida's* rope ladder. Hewitt would be the last sailor rescued by his countrymen. Even though help was right there for the captain, Stubbs would not allow himself to be rescued while he still had men in the water. He would stay right there with them to the end. He waved the ship away, yelling "Get away *Haida*, get clear!" Stubbs also couldn't run the risk of being picked up by the Germans. The captain was dangerously close to *Haida's* propellers as she started up her engines. Stubbs later succumbed to the frigid waters and his body washed ashore at Plouescat Beach.

Two of *Haida's* crew were left on the scramble nets trying to pull Athabaskans from the water. When the ship accelerated speed, the force pulled the two *Haida* crewmen from the nets and into the water. They were rescued by *Haida's* cutter. As the cutter limped slowly homeward with its testy engine cutting in and out, they were buzzed by German aircraft and eventually spotted by a squadron of RAF planes. An air/sea rescue unit was dispatched and the exhausted men were taken onboard and safely returned to Penzance.

Meanwhile at the disaster site, men clung to carley floats, pieces of debris or anything else they could get their hands on. Some of the strongest sailors tried desperately to hold onto other more injured men. Time after time, they would pull someone back from the death grip of the freezing water and encourage them to "hold on." They tried to keep their spirits up by talking. Disbelief gave way to torrents of anger which, in turn, gave way to waves of despair at being left behind. Some sailors screamed obscenities at the sister ship, which had deserted them and left them to die. Prior to *Haida's* return, Captain Stubbs had tried to get the men singing to keep their minds off their perilous situation. They talked of home and of what they would do when they were reunited with their families. With their bodies chilled to the bone and the strength sapped from their limbs, some were resigned to their seemingly hopeless situation and yelled out, "I've had it," or "I can't go on," and slipped quietly away. There was no weapon to fight the hypothermia. All the latest technologies were useless against this subversive force. Silently the loss of body heat and extensive injuries claimed their lives. Their last thoughts must have been of the loved ones they would leave behind. Death to the most extensively injured must have been welcomed over the pain and peril of their futile situation.

Two lifelong rivals found themselves face to face, clinging to the same carley float. Throughout their naval careers, animosity resulted whenever their paths crossed. This time, when recognition dawned on their oil-soaked faces they agreed to put the past behind them and offered forgiveness to one another. A short time later, Chief Petty Officer Bertrand slipped away into silence, leaving Leading Seaman Stanley Rick clinging to the float alone.

Meanwhile, off in the distance the rhythmic 5-second flashing of l'Ile Vierge lighthouse could be seen sending out its warning signals for all those near Brittany's rocky coastline. The lighthouse was so close, yet so far away. Herm Sulkers, noted as a super athlete, thought seriously of trying to swim to shore, but the cold was too debilitating.

The German destroyer *T27* which had been run aground by *Haida* lost seventeen of her sailors from a total crew of 180. The Germans were intending to salvage her, as their naval fleet was diminishing with the final stages of war. After an Allied air attack failed to finish the destruction of *T27*, three British MTBs were sent in to torpedo her in the shallow waters where she lay.

At daybreak, the Elbing destroyer *T24* returned to the battle scene. Dead and unconscious bodies floated on the surface like a minefield of debris. The Athabaskans could not make out who had come to their rescue, were they friend or foe? All they knew was that their survival depended on getting out of the water immediately. They could not feel their arms or legs from the debilitating cold. After several hours of exposure, all were suffering from the effects of hypothermia, and it was a miracle anyone had survived.

The burned and injured sailors picked up by the German *T24* and other rescue vessels were transported to a hospital in Brest for treatment of their injuries. Dr. Eitel W. Marechaux, the physician in charge of treating the injured, remembers being so impressed with the "iron discipline" of the young Canadians. Dr. Marechaux recalled that when it was time for the injured to depart the hospital, the officer in charge lined the Canadian sailors up in the corridor. The officer, on behalf of himself and his fellow crew, then thanked the doctor and his staff for their treatment. "It was heartwarming," said Dr. Marechaux. Then the sailors were whisked away to board a train for their long trek north into Germany and transfer to prison camp.

The enemy, turned rescuers, had retrieved eighty-three sailors from the frigid North Atlantic waters. These men would spend the remainder of the war living in deprivation and mental abuse as POWs, with mock firing squads and the constant threat of the camp's vicious guard dogs. Some, like signalman William Connolly, were to spend extended periods of time in solitary confinement. Bill recalled "never knowing from one day to the next what would become of you," always living in fear.

Meanwhile, *Haida* had rescued forty-four seamen, and the cutter returned to England after eighteen hours with another six survivors. When *Athabaskan's* sister ship had pulled away from the scene, they had left 211 men in the water or otherwise unaccounted for. Ninety-one men washed up on the shores of Brittany in the ensuing hours. They are buried in nine civilian cemeteries scattered along the coastline. Forty-two are identified and another forty-eight unidentified. Thirty-seven bodies were lost at sea. The first torpedo struck between No.1 and No.2 boiler rooms on the port side, causing an enormous explosion. Some in the boiler rooms and below deck were trapped and unable to make it topside. The greatest loss of life occurred among the sailors on that side of the ship, including the annihilated "Y" gun crew.

For the most part, the men who washed ashore were provided with decent Christian burials, except for the three who floated ashore at Ile de Batz. The German commandant ordered that no flowers be placed on their graves. Under the cloak of darkness, no less than 1000 citizens from all over the tiny island defied curfew to attend to the graves. The next morning, the Germans awoke to find flowers piled high on the three fresh mounds of earth.

At Plouescat where fifty-nine of the men washed ashore, they were buried in a mass grave. The Germans did not bury the young sailors, but the Polish conscripts carried out the task. In 1947, long after the war had ended, former *Athabaskan* prisoner of war Lieutenant Dunn Lantier returned to France and ordered the common grave reopened. He identified as many remains as he could through personal effects. The Germans had removed most of their dog tags. Every individual was then re-interred separately. There are twenty-five unknowns in that cemetery.

The tragedy occurred just five days prior to Moe's twentieth birthday, and five weeks before D-Day. It remains one of Canada's largest naval disasters ever.

As was the custom in the Waitson family home, every Sunday morning Pup liked to sit in his favourite easy chair, smoke one of his cigars, read the newspaper and listen to news of the war on the old parlour radio. The morning of Sunday, the 30th of April, he was worn out from the uneasiness that had settled over his family after Alma's nightmare. He played with the dials on the crackling old radio until he could faintly hear the commentator's voice. Then he heard the announcer, speaking in a most sobering tone, tell the listening audience that the famous Tribal destroyer HMCS *Athabaskan* had been sunk off the coast of l'Ile Vierge, France. While they had been sleeping safely in their beds far from the stage of war, fate had changed the dynamics of his family forever. Life would never be the same for any of them again.

ONTARIO

OFFICE OF

THE PRIME MINISTER & PRESIDENT OF THE COUNCIL

February 14, 1945

Dear Mrs. Waitson:

The Government has requested me to convey
to you our deep sympathy in the loss of your
dear son, Able Seaman Maurice Waitson.

We wish to assure you that all members of
the Ontario Government recognize the deep sense
of obligation which the province owes for this
great sacrifice which has been made to preserve
all that we hold dear.

May I express my personal sympathy and the
assurance that those who have paid the supreme
sacrifice will never be forgotten by the people
of Ontario.

Yours sincerely,

George Drew

Mrs. Alma Waitson,
Napanee, Ont.

DND Letter, dated February 1945

Mum's nightmare was now a reality. For sure Maurice was gone. At that point, it was unknown how many were dead and how many had survived, but a mother's instinct is a force to be reckoned with. The listening audience heard about *Haida's* accounts of rescuing some of *Athabaskan's* crew, but the fate of the remainder was unknown.

What every wartime mother fears the most occurred on May 1, 1944, two days after the ship sank, when *the dreaded telegram* arrived from Ottawa addressed to Alma Waitson. An official letter from National Defence in Ottawa, dated the same day, was sent by Canada Post to confirm the contents of the telegram. AB Maurice Waitson was reported missing from the *Athabaskan* after it had been sunk in the English Channel. The letter still left a glimmer of hope, stating there was a possibility of his survival. A number of sailors had been taken prisoner. The names of those prisoners had not been released by the Germans.

All glimmer of hope that Moe might have survived and been taken prisoner was gone by February 1945 when Alma received yet another letter from National Defense. Maurice was now officially listed as "MPD" or Missing Presumed Dead.

Chapter Eight

The Search for Moe

ONE APRIL MORNING IN 2001, I glanced at the copy of *MacLean's* magazine that had just been delivered to my office. A feature article entitled "Maritime Mystery" recounted the brief history of HMCS *Athabaskan* through interviews with one her survivors, Bill Connolly and his wife Vi. According to the article, an upcoming documentary, *Unlucky Lady: The Life and Death of HMCS Athabaskan,* was soon to be featured on the History Channel.

Immediately my early childhood fascination with the story of an uncle who had died in the war flooded my mind. As a very young girl I was enthralled with the family's old green photo album. It was old and worn and tied together with laces. Amidst the pages were tiny black and white photos of various family members. One particular photo of a young lad wearing a naval uniform intrigued me more than the others. The young man was standing on the sidewalk with Big Ben in the background and a coat draped over his arm. My uncle, Maurice Waitson, had been photographed on leave in London, England. I always marveled at the number of men in our family who wore that same uniform of the Canadian Navy.

The most prized article from that old green album frequently fell from between the pages as I carried it to the kitchen table for closer observation. A small brown envelope addressed to my mother, it was Moe's last letter home. I would open, read and then reread that letter time and time again. I knew that he had been a sailor on the HMCS *Athabaskan*. Mother would recoil when I asked about Uncle Moe. She would abruptly say "he died in the war." End of story. "He died in the war!" I knew the memories were too painful for her to speak of her younger brother.

Some years earlier, around the fiftieth anniversary of the sinking, I had contacted Emile Beaudoin, an Athabaskan survivor and co-author of a book entitled *Unlucky Lady: The Life and Death of HMCS Athabaskan*. Although he did not know Moe, we had an engaging conversation as he recalled his experiences aboard *Athabaskan*. However, when I hung up the phone I had no more insight into Moe's life onboard ship than I had before, nor did I have any idea where to go to seek answers.

Now, in 2001, I felt sure that this documentary would shed some light on *Athabaskan's* story and that of her crew. As the documentary aired, a few of the survivors were interviewed, including one extensive conversation with a gentleman whose name was Herm Sulkers. As he continued to talk, the TV screen flashed a photo of Herm with his gun crew, taken on a happier day. Beside him, with the sun shining on his face, was Moe! I was familiar with that picture. Where had I seen that? My fingers flew through the pages of *Unlucky Lady* on my lap, to the photograph of "A" and "B" gun crews. Yes, I hadn't imagined it, that was Mr. Sulkers standing right beside Moe. At the back of the book were pages listing all the sailors on the ship's final mission: their names, military numbers, ranks, ages at the time of disaster, and their hometowns. Their fates were recorded as: MPD (missing presumed dead), *Haida*, (meaning they had been rescued by their countrymen), POW (prisoner of war), or the name of the cemetery they were buried in, provided they were among the fortunate to be identified. Mr. Sulker's domicile was listed as East Kildonan, Manitoba.

Early on the morning of April 16, 2001, I began searching for the name of Sulkers around Winnipeg. Armed with a few telephone numbers, I started to cold call. I had replies such as, "I remember that name, but we are a large family of Sulkers in this area," or "I think he died in the war," or "Call my cousin out in Calgary; he has our family tree. Perhaps he can help." Not to be discouraged, I called the cousin in Calgary. Yes, he knew exactly who I was looking for. The reason I could not locate him in Manitoba was because he now lived in Victoria. He very obligingly gave me Herm's telephone number.

It was still only 10:00 a.m. EST and I knew I had to wait until at least noon our time before I could call to allow for the three hour time difference to the Pacific time zone. The clock never ticked so slowly! Customers became a nuisance. Phone calls and minor tasks were burdensome as I watched the minutes slowly tick by. Not a minute after 12 p.m., I called from the vacant front office in our business. The phone was answered after two or three times.

Hardly had I phrased the words, "Sherry Pringle calling you from Napanee, Ontario," when Herm Sulkers replied with "Moe Waitson, I knew him well!" My family members later found it difficult to believe the immediate recognition resulting simply from the word "Napanee." We would soon discover that everyone on the ship had a nickname and Moe's was "Napanee".

The conversation we had was very informative. Herm was four years older than Moe. They did, in fact, share the same birthday. Once, Herm recalled, the two of them were on KP duty together, cleaning up after lunch with the mundane tasks of washing and drying dishes. Herm told Moe to go topside and throw the slop water from the basin overboard. Minutes later, the thunderous clanking and clashing of silverware was heard below deck, as the utensils splashed into the sea. Moe forgot to check for the cutlery in the murky water of the washbasin. After that, it became a joke with the guys all shouting "Look out for the utensils, Napanee," or "Don't let Napanee near the basin or we will be eating with our fingers."

Herm said he never knew exactly what became of Moe that awful night but was of the understanding that he had been killed instantly with the first explosion. My childhood recollections of being told he had probably been blown to smithereens appeared to be true. The Germans had picked up Herm and the other survivors, left behind by *Haida*, and taken them to hospital for treatment of their burns and injuries. Eventually they were transported to a POW camp in northern Germany where they were to spend the remainder of the war.

I was also told that a very close friend of Moe's, John Fairchild, lived in a small neighbouring town just up the coast of Vancouver Island. John had been the same age as Moe and they had been paired off for shore leave together. Herm volunteered to contact John to establish if he would be in favour of receiving a phone call from me.

It seems that John had been haunted his whole life by the memory of switching gun stations with Moe. My uncle had been posted to "B" guns at the bow, while John was on "X" guns, aft. The gun stations at the bow were cold and wet. Moe had cajoled and badgered John relentlessly into switching gun detail with him. On April 1, 1944, they traded details so Moe could be more comfortable and John could get some peace. Little did they know John's peace of mind was to be short lived.

By the end of our phone conversation, I had agreed to meet Herm Sulkers at the annual *Athabaskan* reunion ceremony on the *Haida,* which at that time was permanently moored at Ontario Place, Toronto. This highly acclaimed warship, now a permanent museum, hosted the memorial service which took place every year on the closest Sunday to the anniversary of the tragedy. It was called "Athabaskan Sunday." We parted ways with his promise to speak to John Fairchild and meet up with me in a couple of week's time.

Chapter Nine
Athabaskan Sunday

ATHABASKAN SUNDAY FELL ON APRIL 29 IN 2001, the exact date of the tragedy. My husband Larry, son Mark and myself drove to Toronto for the ceremony. Other family members joined us there. It was a cool day, but the sun was shining. A formal ceremony was followed by lunch. Chairs were set up beside the *Haida* on the parking lot. My most vivid memory is of singing the Naval Anthem, which is mournful at the best of times, let alone when commemorating the loss of 128 lives. After the service, we were introduced to Herm for the first time. It was exactly fifty-seven years after the disaster. Here we were turning up at such a late date into the lives of the veterans.

Herm gave us a personal tour of the ship, taking us to see the guns at the bow and stern. At "B" gun station he described in great detail how the guns operated. It was here that he got to know Moe, as they had been at the same station working together for seven months. Moe's job was that of a fuse setter, setting the projectiles to explode on impact. Herm's task as gun trainer was to turn the guns to the required angle and position for firing. Herm showed us where the glider bomb had struck the ship just behind them. After the glider attack Moe was transferred to "A" guns and then eventually to "X" guns while Herm had been given another assignment in the communications tower. I was amazed at his agility. He climbed the ladders up and down the decks as though he was still a young man of twenty-three, and there had been no interruption in time.

We were introduced to a number of other veterans. They were all so welcoming and eager to share their personal stories. Everyone pointed to where their "abandon station" was or to where they had been when the orders came from Captain Stubbs. It was truly an amazing day for all of us. Guns and war had never been so interesting.

As we stood on the pavement away from the ship, I watched as my aunt Marion bent over an aging veteran all bundled up in a blanket in his wheelchair. The veteran, accompanied by his son, listened intently as my aunt inquired if Teddy had known Moe? He was unable to speak from the effects of a stroke, but his son Kim told us that he had heard his dad speak of Moe many times. Not only had Teddy Hewitt known Moe, they were best friends, and he had named his first son after his Napanee friend.

Kim continued with the story his dad had repeatedly told him throughout his life, of their last moments together. It seems they had both been blown into the sea after the first explosion between the rear gun stations. After finding one another in the dark, they spotted the *Haida* coming to their rescue. Teddy and Moe tried desperately to swim in the direction of the ship. They were so cold and injured that every stroke seemed to take forever. If only they could make it just that short distance to safety. Finally, after gulping down gallons of salt water laced with oil, losing the feeling in their cold arms, and being overcome by total exhaustion, Moe yelled to Teddy, "Go on. I can't make it!"

Kim said his father insisted that Moe yelled goodbye to him. Teddy Hewitt, battling the numbing cold and heaviness in his arms, struggled to continue swimming until he reached *Haida*'s side. Captain Stubbs helped him up the rope ladder. The ship already had her orders to evacuate. The engines were fired and, as they pulled Teddy up the ladder, Stubbs gave his final command, "Get out of here!" Teddy was the very last sailor to be rescued by *Haida*. The ship steamed ahead and left behind the living and the dead. The destinations of Moe and Teddy were now separated by fate.

After all these years when we had thought Moe had been killed instantly in the explosion, his friend was telling us he had survived the initial blast. The implication of that information was enormous! If Moe had survived the initial blast and succumbed in the water, that meant there was a good chance his body had washed ashore along with many others. If indeed it had, then in all probability he could be buried in one of the unmarked graves in France.

Chapter Ten
The Fairchilds

AS PROMISED, HERM HAD PAVED THE WAY for my contact with John Fairchild. He was not able to attend the memorial service in Toronto on the 29th; however, John said he and his wife Pam would be attending their granddaughter's graduation from Queen's University on the 24th of May. They agreed to stop by for lunch with us on their way to Kingston. I then had a couple of weeks to think about what I needed to ask John about Moe. So afraid I'd forget something important, I composed a long list of questions for him. Finally our decades-old questions would be answered. Besides the obvious battle details and stories of who had seen Moe last and so on, I was more interested in knowing about the man himself. What was he like? Foremost in my mind was the question of whether Moe had a girlfriend. Before the war he had been more intrigued with his sporting activities and his young friends. My mother had always described him as being shy. To never have the opportunity to experience love was beyond anything I could fathom. What if Moe did have a girlfriend in England we never knew about?

As our highly anticipated day arrived, close family members, including Moe's sisters and one remaining brother, arrived early to greet our guests. Minutes later we were laughing and crying as we embraced Moe's dear friend at the door. For decades we had been connected by the circumstance of tragedy.

John regaled the family with stories beyond our wildest expectations. He was a first rate storyteller. His handsome appearance and easy smile warmed everyone's hearts. One could only imagine these two handsome young men of days gone by looking dapper in their naval uniforms walking down the gangway to shore. It did not take us long to understand that John had the same little twinkle of devilry that graced Moe's brown eyes, those same eyes that stared back at me from the pages of Mother's old green album.

Tirelessly he answered all the questions we posed to him. He told us of life onboard ship, of the hard work, the pranks, the fun, and the fear of being in dangerous situations while out on missions. Like a gaggle of geese hovering about their leader, the family followed him about, listening intently and clinging to every word he spoke. John gave us what we needed to know. After lunch we walked along the shores of the Napanee River and up to the falls, pointing out Moe's local fishing haunt behind Gibbards along the way and savouring our precious time together. No one wanted this visit to end. Our ambling provided even more time to spark the memories locked away in John's mind. John's life had been traumatized with the guilt of switching gun detail with Moe shortly before the disaster occurred. We tried to console him with our heart-felt rationalizations that it simply was Moe's time to go, not his.

The young sailors were both nineteen years old. Every Christmas day aboard the *Athabaskan*, it was customary for the youngest sailor to wear the captain's hat and be "Captain for a day." Although Moe and John were both the ship's youngest, John being three months younger, had the honours. The young men were great friends and enjoyed shore leave together. Their youthful exuberance and good looks, all wrapped neatly into a sailor's uniform, made them appealing to the young English girls. In their early days as new recruits, while their crewmembers were enjoying ale at the local pubs, these two young lads had figured out another angle. If they attended the local church functions to meet girls, the girls' mothers would take pity on the boys being so far from home and invite them into their homes for meals. While the other sailors boarded the ship exhausted from their shore leave, John and Moe returned with grins on their faces and their bellies full of home-cooked food.

John had been picked up by the Germans and sent to POW camp, where he had escaped and made his way back to England. He was later hospitalized in northern Scotland with his injuries. One day he recalled being told he had visitors waiting to see him. As he approached, he recognized the two young women he and Moe had been seeing in the south of England between missions. John said one girl's name was Yvonne but was unsure of the other girl's name. He recalled one of them collapsing in tears upon being told Moe was dead. After the war, John had paid a visit to my grandmother in Napanee. He told her about Moe, but omitted the story of the gun switch. Some things are better left unsaid.

Chapter Eleven
France

THROUGH MY CONTINUED CORRESPONDENCE with Herm, I learned the *Athabaskan*'s remains had been located off the coast of France in the fall of 2002. A French marine archeologist, Jacques Ouchakoff, had finally been successful in his decade-long search for the wreck. The ship was not located at the coordinates that had been provided by the navy, but was in fact lying approximately one kilometer from the previously established site. With great excitement over the discovery, the Canadian film-maker Wayne Abbott was determined to produce a second documentary. The idea was to dive to the ship to discover if there was evidence to prove or disprove a "friendly fire" theory.

Controversy has swirled around the mysterious sinking of HMCS *Athabaskan*. Some believed the second explosion was the result of friendly fire from one of the British MTBs which had been thirty miles to the east, in the region of the minefield. Some suggest that the motor-torpedo boat mistakenly took the *Athabaskan* for an enemy ship in the heat of battle. Fuelling the argument is the fact the ship in question, MTB677, is missing one and a half hours of logbook entries for that night. The specific time unaccounted for coincides with the exact time *Athabaskan* was under fire. At the time, three echoes had been detected on the sonar screens of *Haida* and *Athabaskan*. Two of the three were identified as the German Elbings *T24* and *T27*. The Germans reported that there were no other ships from their fleet in the vicinity that night. A school of thought by some of the sailors and authorities is that the second explosion occurred amidships at the No.1 boiler. Some of the drawings of the sinking later rendered by the captive sailors while in prison camp indicate the second explosion (possibly a second torpedo) had a point of entry at that particular boiler location. The mainstream consensus is that the second explosion was caused by internal fire near the magazines, and not a second torpedo. The "friendly fire" theory has since been completely discredited.

Diving for answers to these unknown questions regarding the true nature of the second explosion was foremost in Abbott's mind. His documentary title *The Mysterious Sinking of HMCS Athabaskan* says it all – it is mysterious. There needed to be more definitive answers and closure, once and for all, as to *Athabaskan's* true fate.

The entourage was to include two survivors, Herm Sulkers and Wilf Henrickson; Herm's two sons Paul and Neil; Herm's grandson David; Caroline Scott, wife of

Athabaskan survivor Lieutenant Jack Scott; Jocelyn Turgeon, a naval architect from Ottawa; Barry Gough, a noted naval historian; Mr. Ouchakoff, accompanied by his interpreter; Peter Ward, son of Leslie Ward, the writer sent aboard to write a naval paper for Ottawa; Mark Ward, grandson of Leslie Ward; several international expert divers; the film crew, and my husband Larry and I.

Mark Ward, being one of the expert divers, was given the honour of placing a brass plaque on the wreck. The Canadian Navy donated and inscribed the eighteen-kilogram memorial. The plaque's inscription reads: "At this site, the people of Canada honour the 128 sailors who gave their lives in HMCS *Athabaskan*, sunk in action with the enemy, 29 April, 1944. Protect them whereso'er they go."

Larry and I arranged to fly to Paris, and meet everyone in the port city of Brest, the naval headquarters for Germany's Atlantic fleet during the war. If weather permitted, we might realize the dream of actually being positioned over the exact location of the ship-wreck and witness history being made.

The waters off the coast of France are subject to strong currents that can attain speeds of seven knots. The ship was lying five and a half nautical miles from the coast and in almost three hundred feet of water. Mark Ward had completed extensive specialized training to prepare for this operation. He would be allowed only fifteen minutes on the

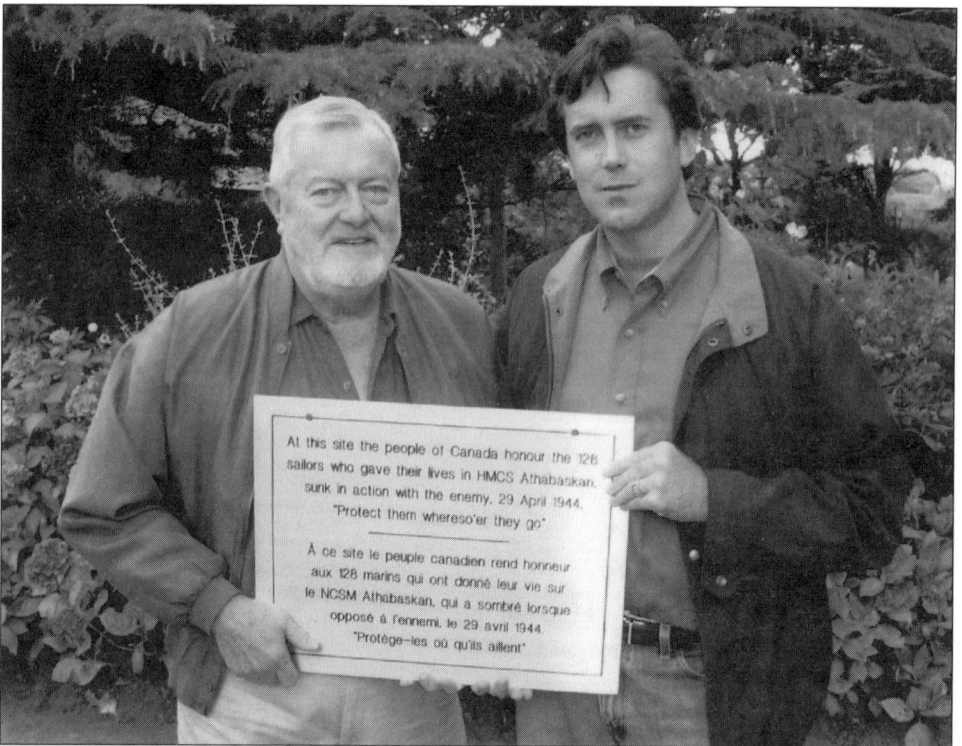

Lieutenant Leslie Ward's son Peter, on left and grandson, diver Mark Ward, hold brass plaque. (courtesy of Mark Ward)

ocean floor due to the intricate nature of a deep dive in cold waters. In that short time, the divers must lay the plaque on the ship and perform the necessary filming. It would be a treacherous dive.

We walked down the little jetty, the same ground where Herm and Wilf had been brought on the morning of the 29th of April, when the enemy had returned to shore at the little village of L'Aber Wrac'h with their captives. The Canadians had been forced to march off this pier and into the little town to await their uncertain fate at the hands of the enemy. One Athabaskan, John McNeil, collapsed and perished from his injuries while marching down the pier. He is the only sailor from *Athabaskan* buried in Landeda cemetery.

Now decades later, we were retracing this same route in reverse, down the jetty to the awaiting vessels to carry us to the site of the wreck. Herm and Wilf eagerly gave us a quick tour to the nearby backyard where they had been corralled until taken away for treatment of their injuries. Herm recalled being in the courtyard for quite a while and seeing a neighbour and her daughter watching them from a window across the street. Eventually the women brought water to the prisoners. They were so grateful for that small act of kindness.

Herm had been given a towel to wipe the oil from his face. While trying to look into a shard of glass from a courtyard window to clean his face, he noticed one of the French women scurry away in horror. When he returned his glance to the glass, he saw what had distressed her. He had not realized how badly burned he was until he tried to wipe the oil from his face, and found that strips of skin had come away.

The seas were calm on the fine, sunny day we ventured forth from the little village of L'Aber Wrac'h. The two dive boats carrying our entourage headed out through the harbour, past the outcropping of rocks. In the distance we could see l'Ile Vierge lighthouse standing guard on Brittany's rugged coastline. The stone lighthouse is the highest in Europe, and the tallest stone lighthouse in the world. Herm was to tell me later that, when the men were in the water waiting to be rescued, they could see the faint beacon from that same lighthouse flash its rhythmic warning to vessels who might approach the rocky coast. Straight ahead of us, across thousands of miles of saltwater lay Canada.

On the trip out everyone was quiet and reflective. Even though everyone had withdrawn into their own thoughts, the quiet was a camouflage for the excitement at what we were about to see and experience on this mission. Chatter on board was hushed and subdued. I concentrated on the experience of visiting the very place where the ship went down and carried away the life of my young uncle. One disastrous moment in time had led all of us onto the same path.

Our two most precious crew, of course, were Wilf and Herm, *Athabaskan's* survivors. We all contemplated what must be going on in their minds as we traveled to the disaster site. Were they recounting their individual tales of survival? Could they feel the cold of the April waters in their bones? Did they have thoughts of their buddies who were lost at sea? They had experienced a nightmarish tragedy almost a lifetime ago; memories like that could never be erased from their minds. The sailors knew the cards could have played differently, with them being amongst those who never returned home. Who is to say who lives and who dies? For this reason, the survivors carried the memory of their fallen comrades as a torch, held high, for the remainder of their lives.

We arrived at our destination on Tuesday, July 22, 2003. The divers entered the water from the craft beside us. We watched as Mark Ward held the heavy plaque high in the air for all of us to see one last time. He then dove to the bottom of the sea. On his person, Mark carried a precious piece of memorabilia. Herm had requested his navy dog tag be placed alongside the ship to be close to his fallen comrades.

After what seemed like hours of anxiously awaiting the group's return, bubbles began breaking the surface, telling us the divers were safe and returning after their perilous mission. The two former sailors, standing guard on the side of the ship, gave Mark a salute when he surfaced. Cheers and applause erupted from everyone as we realized the completion of a very successful mission. Though the ship was found to be in a terrible state of disintegration with its bow in rubble on the ocean floor and its stern not located, Canadian naval architect Jocelyn Turgeon was able to positively identify boiler No.1, lying intact under boiler No.2 on the ocean floor, through photographs taken by the dive crew. Since there is no evidence to support a second torpedo entry at No.1 boiler, it appears to dispel the "friendly fire" theory.

Chapter Twelve
Brignogan-Plages

THE FOLLOWING MORNING we traveled to Brignogan-Plages to visit friends of Herm, a retired colonel from the French military and his wife. We were driven to the local cemetery where our sailors were buried alongside the French civilians. There was one identified grave, and eight unidentified. At every national or patriotic celebration, the French still hold a service at the gravesides in the nine cemeteries where our sailors lie. We were impressed by the immaculate maintenance of the grounds. One couldn't help notice the watering cans hanging near to the water supply for the next visitor to use.

After leaving Canadian flags on the unmarked graves, I sat awhile to contemplate the scene. There was not enough time to visit all nine cemeteries. I was worried about overlooking the one cemetery that could possibly hold Moe's remains. Of course I was staring at the tombstones with "Known Unto God" written on them. How would I know which one might be Moe's? I could be looking at it and never know. Finally I rationalized that, if we only had time to visit three cemeteries, perhaps they were the three I was meant to see. At some point you have to give fate credit. I continued to sit and contemplate and stare at the grave markers. For sure they all looked alike. Was it this one, or that one? We'd come so far for answers not to uncover something. Of course, I knew in my rational mind, Moe might have been one of the thirty-seven bodies not accounted for. I quickly pushed that notion out of my thoughts. No, Teddy was insistent that Moe said goodbye to him in the water, making it probable he is buried on French soil. Herm, being so respectful of his friend had told me, "If Teddy said so, it must be true."

Quietly, I asked God for some kind of sign. Anything would do, just a sign. Please send me a message, I pleaded as I looked up at the headstones all glistening with sunshine. They were all so neatly placed with gravel covering the entire area, surrounded by a white concrete border. Fragrant perennial flowers were planted across the foot of the graves. The setting reminded me of a boxed in area, all neat and tidy, which was set right in the middle of the cemetery.

Time was running out. Our group was conversing at the entrance gate to the grounds, giving me privacy and plenty of opportunity to say goodbye to the sailors. As I raised my head, my eyes immediately rested on the fourth stone from the left. Although it was identical to the others, there, beside the stone was one lonely little bedraggled weed. It seemed to be waving at me in the breeze as if to say "over here!" Who is to say that was a signal or not? I choose to believe it was.

A Sailor of the 1939-1945 War. R.C.N. 29th April, 1941. Known Unto God.
(courtesy of author)

Herm asked me after our time in Brittany together, if any grave spoke to me. Every family member who has had the opportunity to visit these sites experienced the very same phenomenon I was told. Each one chose a specific gravesite and assuredly claimed it as the final resting place of their loved one. I looked at him in surprise and replied "Yes, I know where he is." I feel better now knowing he is buried alongside his comrades. When you are far removed from the scene, in another country, you only envision the negative images of your loved one washing ashore with the tides and being buried on foreign soil, far from home, with no family to grieve at his side. For sixty years our family grieved for a young man of nineteen who had left home, never to return. There was no funeral service, no remains to stand and weep over, no place to lay flowers on a mound of soil, no last post or mournful rendition of "Amazing Grace" filtering the air from bagpipes. He was just an ordinary young man whose life had been cut short by the call to war. The only tangible thing we had to hold on to, was a piece of paper from National Defence in Ottawa stating simply that Moe was "Missing Presumed Dead."

However, knowing first-hand how the French have so lovingly cared for their revered liberators, offers a final sense of peace and resolve. Here there are no barriers between the culture and language of two countries which face one another across thousands of miles of sea. Our fallen countrymen are highly honoured here on French soil.

The Colonel and his wife took us to a point of land on the waterfront where we overlooked the sea in one direction, and the shoreline of their town in the other. Colonel Boisson has long been involved in the Athabaskan Society in Brittany. Madame Boisson described to us the scene that she recalled seeing as a small child, that of the fishing boats dragging the bodies ashore on the days following the disaster. These are the men now buried in the cemetery. Tears filled her eyes as she continued to describe these scenes that had cast a shadow on her youth. After a few moments of quiet contemplation, Herm broke the silence and started to sing "O' Canada." Everyone joined in, standing at attention as if staring at an imaginary maple leaf flag. Together we sang our national anthem, overlooking the quiet harbour of a little French town.

In the 1980s United Press International, datelined Paris, reported that skeletal remains of five young men were discovered by children playing in the sand at the beach on Ile de Batz, France. The five, buried end to end, were determined to all be male with four believed to be between the ages of twenty and twenty-five. The fifth skeleton was believed to be that of a teenager. None of the skeletons showed any visible signs of trauma. Authorities determined the young men had been there possibly for forty years.

Since there were no reports of missing French men, it was highly suspected the remains were those of Athabaskan sailors who had been secretly buried by members of the French Resistance.

Upon inquiring as to the whereabouts of the remains, French authorities disclosed that after a number of years, and prior to the advent of DNA testing, the bones had been destroyed.

Dive to the wreck. (courtesy of author)

"I looked down at Unlucky Lady and she smiled back at me."— Jacques Ouchakoff (courtesy of Wayne Abbott)

Dive to Wreck. (courtesy Wayne Abbott)

Once feared guns. (courtesy Wayne Abbott)

Plouescat Cemetery (courtesy of author)

Chapter Thirteen
Plouescat

TIME IN THE COMPANY OF OUR *ATHABASKAN* companions was quickly coming to a close. Larry and I would spend another day and then head north to the Normandy Beaches, Giverney and finally Paris from where we would fly home. There were still a couple of missions to accomplish. We ferried over to the tiny isle of Ile de Batz, where three of the sailors are buried.

Our final trip was to visit the town of Plouescat, Brittany. It is hard to imagine this tiny, tranquil place being at the centre of gunfire, chaos and tragedy. How could these gentle people have been subjected to such despicable circumstances?

The cemetery here holds the remains of fifty-nine Canadian sailors, including the beloved Captain Stubbs. We meandered amongst the stone markers to pause and contemplate the inscriptions written on them. The headstones of the unidentified sailors read:

Sailor
of the 1939-1945 War
R.C.N.
29th April, 1944
KNOWN UNTO GOD

We continued our walk, reading the markers until one in particular, in perfect alignment with those of his comrades, captured our attention, in front of a stone wall.

L. Ledoux
Sailor, 2nd Class RCNVR
A 4433
HMCS Athabaskan
29th of April, 1944
Age 20
His Mother, Two Sisters and Three Brothers
Weep for Him in Montreal, Canada

Laying Wreath in Plouescat Cemetery. l to r - Colonnel Elie Boisson, unknown, Herm Sulkers, unknown. (courtesty of author)

Plouescat eye witness to explosion on left, talking to Larry Pringle. (courtesty of author)

Original Marker for mass grave in Plouescat Cemetery. *Here Lie 50 Canadian Sailors* (courtesy of Ed Stewart)

Of the sailors buried in Plouescat Cemetery, thirty-four are identified and twenty-five are unidentified. This is the largest burial place for Athabaskans. Every cemetery we had visited was as immaculately groomed as the next. All the markers are lined up in perfect precision; each adorned with flowers or shrubs.

While we strolled among the stones, everyone in deep contemplation, a French woman approached us. After inquiring if we had loved ones here, she pointed in the direction of her childhood home overlooking the sea. Her family had been awakened by the explosion fifty-nine years ago. With watery eyes she described the huge fireball seen in the still-darkened sky five miles out to sea. She continued to describe in vivid detail the vision of bodies washing ashore that morning. The Germans had left our sailors lying exposed on the beaches, while they gave precedence to the burial of their own men. Their sailors had been killed when *Haida* ran their destroyer, *T27*, up on the rocks in the fray that had taken place on the same evening.

The entire entourage of veterans, family, film crew and all those associated with this voyage of discovery collected in the Plouescat cemetery that day for a casual, but emotionally charged memorial service. It was a very fitting ending for our amazing experience. Even the divers and film crew seemed affected by the significance of our purpose there. So long ago, so many young men were never to return to the soil of their Motherland. Their families were never able to properly grieve without the body of their loved one.

Amidst the quiet sanctity of this hallowed ground, we formed a large circle and listened intently as several from our group spoke of the sacrifice of the young men from *Athabaskan* who gave their lives for the ultimate goal of freedom. We gave thanks.

Each member of our group was on their own quest. I was carrying with me the sentiments of my family to find peace for its lost son.

Later on I walked alone, deep in thought, with my toes enjoying the warm July sand of Plouescat beach where the bodies had washed ashore decades ago. Captain Stubbs had been found over there by the wall, I had been told. The carnage was visible in my mind. The wind blew gentle breezes across my face as I stooped to pick up a small stone, worn by the elements. As I stroked its smooth surface between my fingers, I was reminded of the letter of long ago, which is still so vivid in my mind. The sandpipers strutted on the beach, while the gulls squawked overhead as they swooped and dove from the blue sky. On the bluff overlooking the sea, quaint little French country homes stood peacefully as if they had always been there, standing guard over their sacred place in the world. Little dinghies sporting brightly coloured sails were pulled ashore, ready and waiting to go. How could this gorgeous little beach be so peaceful? It belied the terrible scene of death and destruction of long ago. Now it was a place of quiet, beauteous dignity waiting to sparkle with the life of the children who played there. Life is as it should be!

PART II

War Tales: The Veterans Remember

Lieutenant Commander John H. Stubbs
0-70990
Captain HMCS *Athabaskan*
November 6, 1913 – April 29, 1944

Born to British parents in the small mining town of Kaslo, British Columbia, Stubbs got his early sailing experience on nearby Lake Kootenay with the local naval cadets. After completing his education in Victoria where his family had moved, he enlisted in the RCN as a cadet on September 1, 1930.

Upon completion of his naval courses, Stubbs was serving as navigator on the destroyer HMCS *Ottawa* at the onset of war. From that command, he was transferred to HMCS *Assiniboine* as First Lieutenant, eventually becoming her commanding officer.

While onboard *Assiniboine* he was a short distance from HMS *Hood* when the famed British destroyer was sunk by the *Bismarck*. The *Assiniboine* was forced to turn back after giving chase to the German giant, because it was low on fuel.

Commander Stubbs received the Distinguished Service Order for his part in sinking a U-boat after chasing it through a fog bank with his ship's bridge on fire! After serving a one year stint on the staff of the Flag Officer, Newfoundland, he was given what was to become his last assignment.

On November 6, 1943, Stubbs took command of one of Canada's popular new Tribals, HMCS *Athabaskan*. Immediately, he noted a low morale onboard his new ship and declared that he wanted "a strong team spirit between the ranks if Athabaskan is to become a first class fighting ship." He quickly won the admiration and devotion of all

the ship's men. As one of the youngest captains in the Canadian navy, he expertly guided *Athabaskan* on her numerous missions, including those through the perilous Arctic
waters.

The gallant commander of *Athabaskan* refused to be rescued when his ship was torpedoed, but chose to remain in the sea with the men who had served him well. His
honour remains a legend amongst the surviving sailors. It is now up to history to
record his career and assess the life of this brave Canadian mariner who gave the ultimate sacrifice for the cause of freedom.

Commander Stubb's body washed ashore in Plouescat following the disaster. He is
now buried in the cemetery by the same name, where the Bretons lovingly tend his
grave to this day. He was thirty-one years old.

Herman Cornelius Sulkers
V-24660
Able Seaman
May 5, 1920 – November 6, 2006

Herm was nineteen when war broke out. His dreams of becoming a pilot were dashed when the air force recruiting office rejected him. This young lad's spirit was not to be daunted!

If he was not good enough for the air force, he would just go over to the naval recruiting office on Logan Street, in Winnipeg.

The naval office welcomed him with great enthusiasm and he began the enlistment process. First on the agenda was the obligatory medical exam. Herm was in great shape, being very athletic, and he thought the exam would be a cinch. To his further disappointment, he was told they could not accept him because of a condition he had, known as "hammer toe," on his left foot.

In the east end of Winnipeg, where he lived in a poor working class district, there was a gentleman known by the locals as "Doctor." He was not a licensed physician, never having graduated from a medical school; however, he was the only medical help the neighbourhood folk could afford. Herm paid him a visit. It was his unqualified opinion that Herm's hammer toe would be best remedied by an operation. If it was cut open, broken and then reset, it would look corrected. Desperate as he was, Herm agreed to the painful procedure that took several months to heal.

After his recovery, Herm returned to the naval recruiting center and saw the same doctor who had refused him two months prior. The sympathetic doctor told him if he had been willing to endure such a painful procedure to his foot, even though the problem was still not remedied, he deserved to be allowed to enlist. The doctor disregarded the strict regulations and signed the necessary paperwork to admit Herm into the Canadian Navy. He was sent off to be trained and when his assignment came to report to the HMCS *Athabaskan*, whose service number was "G07", it was the proudest day of his young life.

At port in England, after the glider bomb attack, the ship's captain requested a medical doctor be assigned to his vessel. Until that time, the only professional help was one medical orderly who had been run off his feet trying to deal with the wounded. When the ship returned to sea after repairs had been completed, she now carried a new doctor as part of the crew.

After the *Athabaskan* was sunk in April of 1944, Herm was able to grab a piece of deck planking floating in the frigid waters. In the pitch dark of early morning, he sat on the plank and tried hard to keep himself out of the water as much as possible. In the dark he heard someone calling out for help. He paddled his floating device over to investigate the origin of the cries. He found a man close to exhaustion, with both legs broken, trying to keep himself afloat. Herm pulled him onto his plank and rolled him over onto his back. In doing that, he certainly saved the sailor's life. They were both picked up by a German patrol boat a few hours later and taken to shore where they would spend the remainder of the war in a POW camp.

The man Herm saved that day was none other than the ship's doctor, "Doc Savage." He was the same doctor who had bypassed navy regulations and stamped approval on Herm's enlistment documents back home in Winnipeg.

After his capture by the Germans and treatment of his burns in a French hospital, he was placed in a prison camp along with his comrades. Herm was required to march with the entire group of prisoners up the road to another prison camp, where they were being relocated. Marching single-file, they were escorted on both sides by German soldiers brandishing rifles. In the lead was a British airforce officer wearing his long blue coat.

They camped along the roadside in great discomfort one night on their march. One of the prisoners snuck into a farmer's field and dug up some potatoes. Herm and his new buddy, the potato thief, hid the potatoes in their clothing so as not to be noticed with their food. The next day as they marched along with the British officer leading them up the dusty road, a British Hurricane fighter plane flew into view up over the hill immediately in front of them. The officer, not wanting to be mistaken for the enemy, started waving his arms frantically overhead at the plane, hoping the pilot would recognize his uniform. At the same time, the buddy who had stolen the potatoes from the field forgot his hidden treasure and started to wave his arms overhead as well. As he did so, the potatoes fell from under his clothing. He and Herm scrambled to scoop the vegetables from the dirty road just as the Hurricane opened fire, mistaking the marching prisoners for Germans. Six prisoners were killed immediately ahead and behind them, including the British officer. The only thing that had saved them was bending over to salvage their food from the dirt.

When Herm had gone to the enlistment office back home in Winnipeg before he went to war, he had been accompanied by his best friend, Jack Finnie. Jack and Herm were next door neighbours. So close were their homes that the mailman frequently delivered their mail to the wrong household. They were both receiving mail addressed to No.147. To differentiate between the two households, the Sulkers' house was official-ly established to be No.147, and the Finnie's was designated as No.147 1/2. Both young men had wanted to join the air force but Herm was rejected while his young friend Finnie was accepted.

Jack Finnie was flying a mission over occupied Eastern Europe in formation behind the lead plane. As they swooped down to strafe a train, the lead plane dropped a bomb on the locomotive, landing on a boxcar which was transporting a heavy load of explo-sives. Jack's plane caught the full impact of the fiery explosion, which killed him imme-diately. He is buried in a cemetery outside Budapest, Hungary.

Upon his return to Winnipeg after the war, Herm went to pay Jack's mother a visit. Still bitter over the loss of her son, she opened the door to his lifelong friend and declared "Why did YOU have to come home!"

On one of Herm's subsequent trips back to France to visit the graves of his fallen *Athabaskan* comrades, Herm took a little post-memorial excursion to Budapest to pay his respects to Jack Finnie's final resting place. As he departed the cemetery that day, he left behind a little sign adorning his friend Jack's grave that simply read, "147 $^1/_2$."

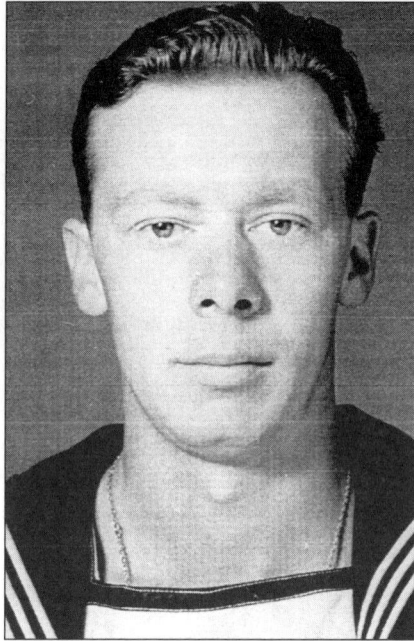

William Connolly
V-40271
Signalman
September 28, 1920 – April 22, 2007

Prior to his assignment to the *Athabaskan*, Bill was stationed on the Norwegian ship, *The King of Norway, the 7th*. The ship had been given to Norway by Franklin D. Roosevelt to use on a lease to own basis. While under power one day a young man fell overboard. Bill had been a lifeguard back home in Ontario so he automatically tied himself to the lifelines, dove overboard and rescued the sailor. Soon after, Bill received an order to see the captain in his cabin.

> "You left your duty station," scolded the captain, to which Bill replied "Yes, I dove in to save that young man." The captain continued on his tirade, reprimanding Bill for leaving his duty station. It seems it is strictly forbidden to perform such an act while on mission in a convoy. "You could endanger every ship traveling in this convoy. Besides, you are a signalman and could have missed some very important signals being sent to us!"

Bill apologized to the captain for abandoning his station. "I have to put you on report but only you and I will know about it," replied the captain. "There will be no medals for your bravery, you understand." Bill certainly was not thinking of being a hero, he was just automatically responding to the situation he had been trained for back home in Hamilton as a lifeguard.

The captain turned his back and poured a water glass full of gin and insisted Bill needed a good stiff drink. Bill hated gin with a passion but didn't want to appear to be ungrateful or to disobey orders. Besides, he thought, maybe the drink would warm him up. Grimacing, he slugged down the gin handed to him and immediately ran to the washroom to upchuck his drink.

The normal punishment for abandoning your duty station is to be sent to the "brig." In this case, the ship being small, it had no brig. Thus, after his scolding the captain sent Bill to remain in his room for a couple of days.

When Bill was assigned duty aboard the *Athabaskan*, he soon discovered there were two other sailors there from his hometown of Hamilton, both named Bill. The three "Bills" from Hamilton all lived within a twelve-block radius of one another but had never met before boarding to serve on the Tribal. The three Hamilton Bills became fast friends, all of them coincidentally were serving in the signal corps.

On the evening of April 28th when the sailors were ordered to return to ship for another mission, Bill Connolly and his Hamilton buddy Willie (Bill Hayes) were sitting together and Willie asked Bill why he was looking so glum? Bill recalls "I told him I thought this was the night we were going to get it!" He continued, "It was a strange feeling and I hadn't had it before."

In the early morning hours when *Athabaskan* was attacked, Bill was sprayed with burning oil with the second explosion. "I looked up and boiling oil was pouring down on everybody. I put my arms over my head and got right over the side. After coming up from under the water I couldn't see. I thought I was blind. Then I remembered I was still wearing my flash hood and it had slipped over my eyes."

He put a lot of distance between himself and the ship as he was worried about the suction action around the sinking ship. In the water he reported "there was lots of panic. There was more confusion in the water than there had been onboard. Nobody could tell who was who." The dead and the survivors were covered in oil as they bobbed in the icy waters. Those still alive were uncertain of rescue or death.

> "Once in the water, I tied onto another sailor not knowing he was dead." That tactic had been part of their training. "When *Haida* began taking on survivors, I started swimming towards her and realized the man with me was dead. I got free of him and started swimming toward the *Haida* again. I was twenty-five feet away when they started pulling in ropes and pulled away.
>
> "It was the most rotten sinking feeling I've ever felt."

Willie Hayes recalled "I was crouched at the side of the ship trying to make up my mind to jump or not when a voice came over the loudspeaker with the order to abandon ship. She was blazing like hell and I jumped. I turned and watched her go down."

Hayes, a thirty-year-old lead coder was rescued by *Haida*. The third Hamilton friend, Bill Stewart is still classified as Missing Presumed Dead.

After being rescued by a German minesweeper and returned to Brest, the survivors were lined up against a wall and a firing squad brought in. Connolly thought to himself "Why would they save us and then kill us?"

The firing squad readied their rifles, aimed them at the sailors but did not pull the trigger. In perfect English the commanding officer said, "That's what'll happen if you try to escape." As a prisoner Bill soon discovered that "if you kept your nose clean, there was no trouble. They didn't mistreat us. They didn't feed us too well either, but they did let the Red Cross packages of food through."

As a signalman, Bill was subjected to interrogation upon arrival at the prison camp. They wanted to know the communication codes, which he informed them wouldn't be of any use to them anyway as they were constantly changing. Sixty-one days in solitary confinement was his punishment for not supplying the answers they wanted.

At a post-war reunion of the Athabaskan Association in Vancouver, a former German naval officer contacted the president of the association at the time, and inquired as to whether he would be welcome to join the reunion activities. He was granted permission to attend.

At the reunion this same naval officer, who had been onboard the German destroyer *T24* which had sunk *Athabaskan*, held up a knife sheath and told his listeners that he had seized a knife from one of the *Athabaskan* crew on the morning of the 29th of April as they plucked the survivors from the water. The spunky lad had also thrust the knife sheath into the hands of the enemy and declared "You might as well have this then, it's no good to me now."

Bill Connolly, on overhearing this story, spoke up to say that young Athabaskan was none other than himself. The officer then recalled how he had kept the knife in his wheelhouse with the intention of returning it one day when the war was over, to the sailor from whom he had confiscated it. Two months later his own ship was sunk and the knife went down with the ship. All that remained was the sheath!

The following year, at the *Athabaskan* reunion, the officer returned a second time. This time, he brought with him the closest replica of that knife that he could find. He presented it to Bill along with a plaque, written entirely in German, which read: *Bill was prisoner of war in Germany until being liberated in 1945.*

Iolanda (Vi) Connolly
"Rosie The Riveter"
April 9, 1923

Vi Connolly was the Canadian war bride of Bill Connolly. When the call went out for Canadian women to come and work at the factories filling the vacancies left by the men overseas, Vi didn't hesitate. She left her comfortable job with the telephone company and went to work at Sawyer- Massey-Argus. Before the war, the company had manufactured farm implements.

Vi's job entailed drilling holes in five-inch-thick steel plates that were to become mounts for guns aboard destroyers such as the *Athabaskan*. She was the renowned Canadian "Rosie the Riveter." The drill she operated was state of the art and also top secret. When she was photographed for the "Rosie" posters, she was moved away from her secret machine and placed in a different setting.

When the ship sank, Vi did not know what had happened to Bill. His name did not appear on the list of crew rescued by *Haida*. Was he dead or being held as a prisoner of war? The Germans had not released the names of their captives, in defiance of the Geneva Convention regulations. It was not until three months later, after the Red Cross intervened to force the Germans into releasing the names of their captives, that Vi got her answer.

At home in Hamilton, Vi was living with her in-laws. They had a wonderful postman who would ring the doorbell twice as a signal to Vi or a member of the Connolly family that he had delivered a letter regarding Bill. On this particular day, he had a card from

Bill addressed to Vi. Along his route, he happily informed her neighbours and friends that he was carrying this precious message to Vi. When he rang twice at the Connolly door, Vi's mother-in-law opened it to find not only the postman, but a dozen men and women, friends and neighbours, who had followed him down the street as if he were the Pied Piper, waving little flags and yelling, "Bill's alive. He's alive!" Word finally reached Vi at the plant. Her boss let her go early that day to celebrate Bill's survival.

The message arrived in the form of a preprinted postcard with little check boxes beside the lines. He had checked the box marked "prisoner of war" and signed his name at the bottom of the card. The war separated Bill and Vi for three and a half years.

John W. Fairchild
V-4709
Gunner
August 18, 1924

As the Fairchild household was coming to life on the morning of April 30, 1944, the announcer on the radio station was soberly telling his listening audience about the HMCS *Athabaskan* being torpedoed off the coast of France. The Fairchilds were filled with grief in the uncertainty of John's fate. The announcer said the *Haida* had rescued some of the Athabaskans, but what was the fate and the condition of the remainder of the crew? With great despair about the tragedy, they were quietly discussing the circumstances of the event when John's sister walked into the room after waking from her night's sleep and inquired as to why everyone was so upset. Upon hearing the news, she very calmly stated that "John is okay. I know because I saw him in my dream last night and he is alive. He had a little light shining off the top of his head like a halo. Don't worry, John is alive!" John's parents regarded her as being dazed from her sleep.

John had been picked up by the Germans in the aftermath of the sinking. His family would not be informed of his whereabouts for quite some time, just like the families of the other prisoners of war.

As the war was nearing its end, the enemy decided to move the prisoners from one camp to another further north. On being told they would have a long march to the new location John decided there was no way he was going along. With two fellow

Athabaskans, he hid out in the loft of one of the camp buildings, along with three Norwegian prisoners.

A German soldier came into the barn, climbed the stairs into the loft where the men lay in hiding in the attic's pink insulation and repeatedly thrust his bayonet into the insulation and fired his rifle into the rafters. One of the frightened Norwegians, who had been hiding by the chimney, poked his head out startling the German. The startled soldier lost his balance and tumbling backward, fell through the rafters onto the cement floor below, seriously injuring himself. The Norwegians fled from their secret place, running out into the camp yard and were immediately shot down. The Canadian escapees remained hidden there for a while until the German voices stopped and the coast was clear, then, they slipped quietly away from the camp.

The three Athabaskans made their way to a nearby civilian internment camp. After they were fed, the local French priest offered John his spare robe for disguise. It was tempting for sure, but John knew the ramifications only too well for being caught out of uniform. Regrettably he declined the priest's kind offer, thinking it safer to make his way to Brussels in what remained of his uniform so as not to be mistaken for a deserter and shot on the spot. What comprised John's uniform at that moment was a French naval tee shirt, a British army battle jacket and the equivalent of sweat pants.

Lying on his belly on a nearby hilltop, the new escapee watched as the convoy of fellow prisoners marched from camp heading east, toward their new location. An approaching Red Cross truck following the convoy, stopped to talk to him on the road but refused him a lift because they were monitoring the relocation of the prisoners. The paymaster gave him some British pounds to sustain him for a couple of days until he could reach safety in Brussels. John parted company with the Red Cross after being promised officials in Brussels would be radioed with the news that he was on his way. Arrangements would be made in Brussels for his safe return to England.

Eventually John arrived safely in Brussels. Freedom was a tough act in itself. As were all the incarcerated Athabaskans, he was tired, hungry and suffering malnutrition. All of that did not deter a young, virile sailor from being enticed into the clutches of brothel ladies. John was not sure it was his physique that was the main attraction for the ladies or the fact that he was in possession of British currency. For three days and three nights the young sailor remained at the "house of ill repute" before making his way to the designated safety of the authorities in Brussels, who had been patiently awaiting his arrival.

Those three days spent in self-appointed exile, could have been a costly mistake for John, as he could have been labeled "AWOL." At any rate the authorities turned a blind eye to his unknown whereabouts and drove him to the airstrip in Brussels. After suffering a year of indignities at the prison camp, he was surprised when taken out onto the airstrip, his pants were pulled down and he was deloused. Upon safe arrival at the airport in Croydon, England, he was to suffer the same humiliation for a second time that day. John was then sent on to Scotland by train to a hospital for treatment of his injuries.

Long after the war was over and John had married his Welsh bride Pamela, they spent part of the year living in Wales. John was interested in researching his family tree with its roots steeped in England's history. Together, John and Pam discovered there was a Peter Fairchild living in a neighbouring town. One bright day they set out to make the acquaintance of Peter and see if there was any family connection. They hesitated a little at the door wondering how they would be received. Perhaps they were intruding on this total stranger. Moments later a gentleman opened the door to greet the callers. Not only was the gentleman of the house Peter Fairchild, but he looked amazingly similar to John. Both were tall, handsome, blond, curly-headed, lively men with a zealous penchant for life.

They spent the entire day together visiting. It was not long before the distant cousins began to talk of war. The tone of their conversation quickly changed from exuberant to reminiscent. Peter inquired of John's whereabouts during the course of the war. John quickly responded with "I was in the Canadian Navy," to which Peter countered "I saw the *Athabaskan* blown up!"

"If you saw the *Athabaskan* blown up, you must have been part of the 10th Flotilla because the incident happened five miles from shore." "I was," came the reply.

Sydney A. Cottrell
V-18362
November 1920 – April 29, 1944

Sydney Cottrell was a young man of twenty-one when he enlisted in the navy in 1941. After his recruitment and training in various establishments from Kingston to Halifax and Scotland, Cottrell was called to serve aboard the HMCS *Trillium* on October 14, 1941, shortly after the ship's commissioning. By March of 1942, Cottrell had earned the rank of Able Seaman, his promotion from Ordinary Seaman.

By July 1942, he was sent back to Halifax until September of that year. He enjoyed a twenty-eight day leave and was then sent to *Niobe* in Scotland. Here he was to await the completion of HMCS *Athabaskan*. During this period of time, many Athabaskans were sent on training courses. Cottrell is recorded to have taken a ten-day course on firefighting at Shearness and an additional two week course on the *Osprey*.

According to survivor Herm Sulkers, it is thought that Cottrell was assigned to work at the ammunition supply for "Y" gun. Since "Y" gun was the site of the first torpedo hit, with only one survivor, it is thought Cottrell was probably blown off the ship with the force of the explosion.

This young man from Trenton, Ontario was one of the lifeless sailors whose body washed ashore onto Plouescat Beach in the ensuing hours. He is buried in the cemetery there.

Ralph Frayne
HMCS *Haida*
V386
"B" Gun
March 9, 1925

At the age of fourteen, Ralph joined the army. After a brief period he was transferred to the merchant navy and finally the Canadian navy where he finished his war service. He completed a combined operations course and then spent time on a corvette before being assigned to HMCS *Haida* upon her commissioning.

As a member of "B" gun crew, he described how the crew on the bridge kept the gunners informed on what was happening so they could prepare their guns for positioning and firing.

Ralph was the youngest crewmember on *Haida* for several months after her commissioning, until a young British lad arrived on the scene and upstaged his title.

The Haidans and Athabaskans had a very close relationship. It was not uncommon to spend a mealtime on the other's ship. Ralph had friends on *Athabaskan* and sometimes found himself eating in their mess. No other Tribals shared the intense bond that the crew of these two Tribals enjoyed. Ralph described *Athabaskan* as a "happy ship, unlucky, but happy."

One of Ralph's friends, "Salty" Gosnell was among the casualties from the glider bomb attack on *Athabaskan* in the Bay of Biscay.

On the night of April 28, 1944, as the two ships set out from Plymouth, Ralph remembered it was "just another night, nothing extraordinary, just another night." Still hyped up from the victory of two nights past, when they had helped to sink the German *T29*, he and his comrades were hoping to meet resistance.

When *Haida* witnessed the explosion on *Athabaskan* and returned to assess the situation, Ralph recalled seeing the numerous bobbing lights on the survival gear of the seamen. As the ship settled downwind of the men and debris, the crewmembers from the torpedo stations on the lower deck assisted in retrieving the survivors. Rescue attempts were difficult because the ship kept drifting away from the survivors who were struggling to reach them.

Ralph recalled how he and a young French Canadian chap from his crew started to head toward the retrieval area to help and were quickly stopped by the Petty Officer and ordered back to their stations. All seamen on the *Haida* were to remain at their stations to be ready for any hostile activity that might occur. The guns remained "At the ready."

The atmosphere onboard HMCS *Haida* as she returned to port in the early morning hours of April 29, was very somber. The young Canadian men aboard the Tribals were favourites of the dockyard maties, who worked the English ports. It was customary for the maties to line the docks and welcome home the ships from their missions. As their battle ensign flew and the maties turned out to greet the Haidans, they felt anything but victorious. The hoots and yells expressed on previous missions, were replaced by sober faces as they mourned the fate of their Tribal companions.

Ralph lost another *Athabaskan* friend that night. His friend Jerry was below deck and unable to make it safely out. He is among the Missing Presumed Dead.

Simon Muzyka
22045
HMCS *Haida*
Electrical Artificer
April 10, 1921

Simon witnessed *Athabaskan's* second explosion from his position on *Haida's* quarter-deck. The explosion was so violent, that "stuff was flying through the air."

He had just hung up the phone after reporting to the bridge from the DC pistol room, after checking on No. 3 boiler room. As he walked out on to the port deck, the rescue operation of the Athabaskans was already underway.

"I stopped to help pull a man on to the deck when someone below on the scramble net yelled to 'give me a hand, they're slippery.' So I went down a few rungs down and pulled and pushed as they were handed up from below."

While clinging precariously to the scramble net, Simon watched helplessly as one of the rescued Athabaskans he'd just helped pull from the icy Channel waters fell past him and back into the sea. The lad's grip on the ladder had proved impossible because his hands were slick with oil.

Soon after Simon's involvement with the rescue attempts, orders were given over the loudspeaker to get off the scramble nets and prepare for evacuation. All the carley floats were thrown into the water for the Athabaskans to use for lifesaving devices. The whaler and the motor cutter had been lowered over *Haida's* starboard side, while the rescue was being carried out on the port side. As Simon was making his way forward on the starboard side, toward the ship's bow, he noticed that the whaler was still attached with a line. It was being dragged, bumping, alongside the ship. *Haida* was now traveling at high speeds and the whaler was filling up with water. The line had to be cut to free the whaler. A number of *Athabaskan* lives might have been saved had it not been for the now useless whaler.

Visions of *T29* ablaze on the shore and the five-second flashes from l'Ile Vierge lighthouse were imprinted on Simon's memory as *Haida* pulled away from the tragedy.

Haida radioed C-in-C in Plymouth and requested an aircraft escort. Fog had set in on England's shores and the planes were unable to take off. An enemy plane circled the battle's survivor, dropped a bomb in the ocean and left.

Daylight was fast approaching as *Haida* made her way to the safety of home port. Simon recalled the feeling of relief upon seeing the two destroyers that C-in-C had sent out to escort *Haida*. "It was the happiest sight to see—because we were all out of ammunition and only had practice shells left!"

Battle and rescue had left the *Haida* covered in the stench of cordite and oil. Major cleanup began of the oil-covered decks. Personal effects, such as blankets and hammocks, used to wrap the rescued Athabaskans in, had to be cleaned and sorted. With the mundane tasks of reorganizing the ship came the realization that, "war was serious!"

Glen MacNeill
V-49124
Gunner
December 10, 1923

AB Glen MacNeill was only a crewmember of the *Athabaskan* for six weeks prior to her final mission. He had been assigned to corvettes running convoy from Boston to Halifax, Newfoundland and finally Londenderry. His position on the new Tribal was that of an anti-aircraft gunner, operating the pom poms situated aft of midship. At his station he searched the skies for enemy aircraft.

In the predawn hours of the 29th, he was blown quite literally sky high, thirty feet into the air, and crashed back onto the steel deck of the ship. He immediately lost consciousness from the blow. When he came to, the ship was already sinking stern first. He fell backwards and slid along the deck, bumping into objects of all descriptions and into the water. He recalls there not being much turbulence in the water; no swirling was observed around the sinking ship; however, a terrible racket disturbed the already unsettled darkness as everything broke loose from its restraints. Equipment of every description: naval paraphernalia, guns, mounts, and even the piano, could be heard adding to the clamor of the sinking ship. Glen credits the new Mae West lifejacket with saving his life. "When you pulled on the chin strap of the jacket hood, the little light on top was activated."

He clung to a carley float until being picked up by the Germans. He too spent the remainder of the war as a prisoner. He recalled trading cigarettes with the guards of the camp in exchange for extra potatoes and onions. The malnourished men had to pro-vide their own sustenance with whatever food they could scavenge. The food from their Red Cross parcels would be added to their meager assortment of vegetables to be cooked on a camp stove. On the occasion that a local cow or horse was killed by gun-fire, they would be treated to some "red meat."

Lieutenant Jack Scott
0-65660
Lieutenant in Charge of Gunnery
March 13, 1922 – October 19, 1989

Halifax naval architect William Scott heard the disastrous news that his son's ship had been sunk on the BBC news the morning of April 30, 1944.

As the bodies began washing ashore at Plouescat, on Brittany's coastline, the Germans removed their personal effects, including dog tags, papers, watches and rings. Among the German soldiers was a Polish recruit. He found letters addressed to Lieutenant Jack Scott in the pockets on one of the bodies. The Pole, thinking the papers were of military value turned them over to a Frenchman assisting with the dead, instead of the German authorities. That Frenchman was René Montfort of Plouescat, who kept the letters hidden from the Germans. They busied themselves with the task of burying the dead.

After the war was over Monsieur Montfort, burdened by his hidden documents, sent a letter of condolence to William Scott on the death of his son. Montfort starts his letter by saying: "Now that my relations with America are established, I find it my duty to give you the information respecting the burial of Sub. Lt. J.W. Scott, in the Plouescat cemetery." The letter, dated July 2, 1945, informs William that he is in possession of letters of Jack's, whose body washed ashore and is now buried in Plouescat. Mr. Monfort went on to recall that German orders to refuse Christian burial to the sailors had been defied, and indeed a service had taken place at the mass grave. To further defy the

German authority, the local French villagers had covered the grave with mounds of flowers.

His letter offering sympathies to a grieving father reads, "Our sincere sympathy is with you. The sacrifice of your son and his companions is very dear to us, as we all know that it is due to such men that we now have our liberty and that it is from Canada." It was signed René Montfort.

In response to the letter, Mr. Scott replied to Mr. Montfort and also the Department of National Defence in Ottawa, stating that he was happy to report his son was not dead, but very much alive and recovering from his burns. Scott, suffering critical burn injuries, had been hospitalized in the United Kingdom prior to his return to Canada. It seems Lieutenant A.R. Nash, Jack's cabin mate, had mistakenly put Jack's coat on when the call to abandon ship had been received. While Nash's body had washed ashore at Plouescat, William's twenty-two-year-old son, Lieutenant Jack Scott, had been the only *Athabaskan* officer rescued by *Haida*. From that initial BBC broadcast which reported Lieutenant Scott's rescue, William Scott had the relief of knowing his son was safe.

In a subsequent post-war visit to France, Lieutenant Jack Scott had the opportunity to meet with local officials and discuss the intrigue surrounding the case of Jack's mistaken identity.

Wilfred O. Henrickson
V-16590
Submarine Detector
October 12, 1923 – April 26, 2009

AB Wilf Henrickson was one of the sailors picked up by a German minesweeper after the disaster on the 29th. As they were brought to shore at L'Aber Wrac'h, Brittany, the German army took over the captives. The men were all lined up against a stone wall with submachine guns pointed at them. They did not know what would happen to them. Were they all to be shot? It was not long before an old army truck pulled up and stopped beside them. The sailors were separated into two groups and the truck took off to an unknown destination with half of the men in the back. The remainder were taken to a hospital in Brest for treatment of their burns and injuries.

Wilf was one of the badly injured, suffering third degree burns to his face and hands. He recalls lying on the hospital cot while three German doctors and several nurses surrounded his bed, trying to decide how best to treat his wounds. He had been near a boiler that had exploded on the ship during the catastrophe. His eyelids were so burned that he couldn't see. Consequently, his entire head was bandaged, including his eyes and face, with only one small hole left at the corner of his mouth for a straw to pass through for nourishment. The new Canadian captives were held in Brest for a ten-day period.

In the next room on their hospital floor were the injured German sailors from the previous night's encounter, as well as the injured from the night of the 26th when the

Canadians had sunk *T29*. The men were at the mercy of their captors, including the medical assistants. One of the nurses took no measures to minimize the pain and discomfort of her new charges. She would roughly jerk their bandages off one by one working in a circle about the room. After each burned patient had their bandages removed, she would go to the next and do the same. Once around the room, she would then start to re-bandage a patient, leaving the others with burns exposed to the air for long periods of time, heightening their pain and discomfort. They soon learned the reason why. Her brother had been one of the German sailors killed by them when *T29* was sunk.

After their initial hospital stay, the injured men were boarded onto a train heading north. As Wilf sat with his head still bandaged and unable to see, the train was stopped. He asked his friend Herm, sitting beside him, why they had stopped. Herm replied that French women had boarded the train and were passing out freshly baked bread to the young men. It was a very warm act of kindness that would remain embedded in their memories.

They were taken to a convent in Orleans, France, where the nuns took over their convalescence for another two months. The courtyard of the convent was divided in two by a fence. One side was for the use of the nuns and the other for the sailors. Wilf's care at the convent was conducted by a French doctor who had been captured in North Africa. He did not have much in the way of medical supplies, however Wilf credits him with minimizing his burn injuries with the use of a septic pencil.

When their convalescence at the convent was over, the men were finally shipped out to a prisoner of war camp in Northern Germany. There were two prison camps the sailors were taken to, Marlag and Milag Nord. Wilf hid out and stayed behind while his fellow Canadian sailors marched from Marlag to Milag Nord. They were being relocated to a merchant navy camp. He went undetected because, when he spoke in his native Swedish tongue, the German soldiers mistook him for one of the Norwegian prisoners.

A couple of days before the camp was liberated, someone spotted two armed guards sitting atop guard posts in the safety zone surrounding the camp. No one was permitted to be in that zone. Since the guards had all left the camp three days prior, it was reported to the German naval captain who had remained behind to take care of the inmates.

The naval captain in turn chased the soldiers away, across the road and into an abandoned house. The next day the prisoners noted the roof was missing off the house. They were certain it had been there initially, as they couldn't possibly have imagined it. When the British later freed the prisoners, they told them the armed guards had not gone unnoticed. They had been watching the guards from a distance but could not fire because of the close proximity to the captive sailors. Once the German officer had chased the soldiers across the road, away from the camp, they were fair game. The British then opened fire on the farmhouse, shooting and throwing grenades, thus killing the soldiers who had been hiding out in the attic. Their liberators were the Scottish Highlanders.

John George "Buck" Parsons
V18056
Leading Seaman
December 8, 1917 – May 17, 1996

Buck Parsons had luck on his side. He had joined the navy with his older brother Harry. Before his assignment as a rating onboard HMCS *Athabaskan,* he had escaped the sinking of three ships on prior duties; the *Spikenard*, the *Louisburg* and the *St. Croix*. On each occasion Buck had been assigned to a new vessel prior to the previous one being sunk. Not only had Buck managed to stay out of harm's way on the warships but once, while on leave in England, he had set out to visit his grandmother but missed the first train. That train was strafed by the enemy and several passengers were killed.

Parson's youngest brother John was lost at sea when the ship he was assigned to, the HMCS *Raccoon*, was sunk by a German U-boat in North American waters within sight of the St. Lawrence River shores, in September of 1942.

In August of 1943 when *Athabaskan* was attacked by the glider bomb, Buck was an after-turret gunner, thereby missing the point of impact which occurred forward in the ship.

As *Athabaskan* was engaging in her final battle of April 29, 1944, Parsons was now captain of "A" guns and situated at the bow. On this occasion, the torpedo struck near the aft guns.

Parsons had to be forcibly removed from his position at "A" gun by his crew. He was still firing round after round as the ship was sinking lower into the sea. His crewmates rescued him and tossed him overboard. Later, when asked about being taken from his gun position, he replied "I've already lost a brother at sea in this war." He continued, "I figure that it is going to take a lot of shooting to even up for that."

In the water Parsons and Glen Newlove were clinging together. Parsons asked to be rolled over onto his back so he could work at trying to activate the light on his gear. Bruce Kettles, who had joined the twosome, had to wrap his legs around Parsons to keep him from being flipped over onto his stomach by the rolling waves. When he eventually managed to get the light operable, he exclaimed, "I'll be damned, it works." For a brief moment in the midst of the chaos, the threesome enjoyed a laugh.

Parsons was one of the forty-four Athabaskans rescued by HMCS *Haida*. The twenty-six-year-old sailor traveled home to Halifax aboard the hospital ship *Lady Nelson* to his anxiously waiting young wife and new son.

Lieutenant Robin Hayward
0-31940
Navigating Officer
December 1, 1920 – September 22, 2006

Born in Duncan, B.C. to British parents, Robin Hayward was a cadet-in-training on the *Conway*. In 1939, he was one of twelve cadets selected to attend the Royal battleship *Nelson*. One year later he found himself onboard the HMS destroyer *Nelson*, as part of Lord Louis Montbatten's famous Fifth Destroyer Flotilla. After the British ship was damaged by torpedo fire while on escort duty with a convoy, Hayward was enrolled in gunnery and navigation schools. Sub-Lieutenant Hayward spent the summer of 1942 at home in British Columbia on leave.

By the ripe young age of twenty-two, Hayward was already a seasoned and accomplished sailor when he joined the officers and crew of HMCS *Athabaskan* as their navigating officer. Already carved into his psyche was the experience of surviving two former torpedo attacks on previous ships.

In his wartime diary, Hayward recalled that the second torpedo hit occurred while the ship's company were already "in the act of preparing to abandon ship." He was picked up by a German minesweeper several hours after entering the water and given a hot shower, four cups of coffee and a piece of bread and jam, which he found he could not eat. He felt "dazed and mystified at the sequence of events, hardly realizing at the time that I was a prisoner of war. But it did not take long to realize that I was not free to do as I chose." Traveling to the French coast the minesweeper was the last ship in a line-up of three, motoring in single file, transporting their captured enemies to *terra firma*.

The first three weeks of his incarceration were not pleasant. "I think each man must have been questioned about fifteen times if not more." Before the arrival of the first Red Cross parcels, the prisoners were subjected to German prison cuisine. Breakfast consisted of two pieces of bread and a cup of herb tea. Lunch was the only hot meal, consisting of soup and potatoes, or cream of wheat and potatoes. Supper consisted of two pieces of bread and butter or bread and jam.

Three weeks later, the first Red Cross parcels finally arrived. "It was almost like Christmas or a big day at school receiving a tuck parcel." Although Hayward was still restricted to solitary confinement, "life once more seemed worth living." Exercise was allowed two to three times daily. By exercising and using the "heads," the men could determine who was still in their huts and who was still being interrogated.

"Saturday, 17th of June, was a red letter day in our camp life. Dunn, [Lieutenant-Commander Dunn Lantier] and I spoke to each other for the first time since we were in Brest on our way down to the camp Marlag "O." It seemed marvelous being once more amongst Englishmen and being able to talk without being overheard by a guard or 'Posten' as they are now known."

Hayward and Dunn were introduced to the paymaster and given some Red Cross clothes and given a tour of the camp. It became evident that Linton, the paymaster, was the most powerful man in the camp.

During the first few days the newest prisoners talked non-stop to the other Canadian prisoners who wanted to know all the details about the *Athabaskan* being sunk and the events that ensued. Not knowing the fate of the rest of the crew or that of their captain, the thoughts of their comrades were never far from their minds. Theories and rumours were plentiful.

Hayward noted this speculation in his diary of August 26, 1944: "Some very bad news was received today, through Lt. Lloyd-Davis, a fellow Canadian through his wife, asking if Lt. Commander Stubbs had arrived in the camp. This of course upset us all because we all thought that he had got home safely. Most of us don't believe it, as two of the seamen helped him up the '*Haida* ship's side', so they say. It remains to be seen whether he got home or not. The Germans say his body was washed up on the Finnish coast."

Life in Marlag "O" was much preferred to the life the other Athabaskans endured in Marlag "M". The Canadian imprisoned officers played basketball, softball and a ship game known as "deck tennis." Plays and exhibitions were part of their scheduled activities.

There were however, escapes and escape attempts from the Marlag camps.

"Five have escaped from this camp and 'Marlag M' since the camps were started three years ago. Over two dozen have escaped but have been recaptured again. Only one other attempt has been made since we joined the camp, and that was in June on a bath party using a dummy

but was unfortunately discovered. We go up to the bathhouse once a week in parties of forty to have a shower. The men escaping hid in the bathhouse with 'Little Albert,' as the dummy was known, which was held up between the men. The face was made of clay and its eyes even opened and closed. This was used successfully four or five times for escapes. The German Posten that discovered it received the Iron Cross and a week's leave."

Hayward survived his prison ordeal to return home to British Columbia. Lieutenant Robin Hayward's arrival in Canada was bittersweet, as his mother had passed away just a few months prior to her son's release from prison camp. Thoughts of being reunited with his family had helped him survive his ordeal from the sinking ship and subsequent incarceration, only to discover he would never see his mother again!

Decades later in Duncan, B.C., Hayward and his wife were enjoying lunch one sunny day at the Maple Bay Yacht Club. Another couple sat down at their table to join them for lunch. They chatted away and Hayward noted the new acquaintance had a heavy German accent. In the course of their conversation, the German told the Haywards that he was on the ship that sank the *Athabaskan*.

Johannes (John) Ulhmann
Kriegsmarine
Navigator
February 6, 1923

What was life like as a German sailor in World War II? Was life any different from other young men during wartime? On both sides of the Atlantic, men were obeying the call to defend their country by joining the military, naval and air services. In Germany it was no different. John Ulhmann was a lad of seventeen when he enlisted in the German navy. His older brother had already enlisted in the same service, being stationed with the coastal artillery, protecting important arteries.

Upon enlistment, John was sent to serve on the German destroyer *Z23*, running missions in the Baltic, and on the western coast of France. After spending time on this destroyer, he was sent off to be trained as a navigator. From navigation school, he was sent to serve as navigator on the German destroyer *Z14*, running missions in the Baltic Sea and off the western coast of Norway.

Life as a young sailor was full of the camaraderie shared with close friends. Three hundred men usually comprised the complement of crew on a German destroyer. The duties of these ships entailed escorting the larger battleships and cruisers out into the waters in the North Atlantic, while protecting the coast.

On several occasions, *Z23* escorted the *Scharnhorst* out and back into the safety of German waters. Once, while accompanying *Scharnhorst*, they entered the bay of Brest, France, where a British plane was shot down trying to attack them. Four of the airmen climbed safely out of the plane which had landed in the water not far from *Z23*. The captain of *Z23* immediately shouted the orders "Launch boat to rescue the British airmen!" Ulhmann stated, "For us, it was a matter of course to rescue an airman or seaman, regardless of their country."

Although Uhlmann never saw the British ship *Hood*, nor HMCS *Athabaskan* on the waters, he did participate in an escort for the mighty *Bismarck*. "It really was the pride of the German Navy." The *Bismarck* was dispatched through the Danish Islands, into Skagerak along the Norwegian coast and then westward into the Atlantic.

Ulhmann was once again sent back to navigation school in East Germany. As the Russians steadily advanced westward, he and the other sailors were ordered to hang up the blue uniforms of the navy, and don the grey uniforms of the German army. They were sent out to fight the Russians when Uhlmann was wounded.

He spent two weeks in hospital and was released early with his wounds still open, because the hospital needed the space for more urgent cases. Uhlmann was home recuperating from his ordeal when armistice was declared. At the end of the war, John Uhlmann emigrated to Canada where he continues to live with his German-born wife.

The naval monument in Kiel, Germany, at the entrance of the Kiel fjord and the Baltic Sea is 85 metres tall. Originally built as a memorial to the sailors of the Imperial German Navy who died in WWI, it was later dedicated to seamen of any country who died in the line of duty. (courtesy John Uhlmann)

Ernest Takalo
V-33953
Stoker
September 13, 1924

"The evening of April 28, we were tied up on a buoy alongside HMCS *Haida*. Our cat Ginger kept jumping over to the *Haida* and the seamen kept throwing her back. This kept up until the *Haida* was too far away. We took this as a very bad omen.

The four of us [crewmates] went down to the No.2 boiler room to start our watch at 8:00 p.m. Our watches were four hours on and four hours off. At midnight we went to our defense station to be very close to our action station. Just before 4:00 a.m. action stations were sounded. Bill and I went down to our lower deck position to pass ammunition to "B" gun. The first torpedo hit the stern and the ship stopped. The captain gave us orders to go to our "abandon ship station" at the break of the fo'c'sle. I was under the anti-aircraft gun platform. I hit my head on the platform and, as I was flying through the air, I could see the brush marks on the paint on the side of the ship, the flash was so bright.

I had a concussion and then landed on the deck. My partner was blown off the ship. I woke later and went to the railing to see my ship-mates in the water. I didn't want to jump on them so I went down the ladder to the main deck. I stepped over the railing and into the cold, oily water. I swam away from the ship and then came back to hang onto a carley float. At that time the ship was sinking.

Later the HMCS *Haida* came in the middle of the blinking lights on our new life jackets. I swam to the ship and got onto the scramble nets. Some *Haida* crew were on the nets and helping us up. It was hard as we were covered with oil. When we got on deck they stripped our clothes off and put blankets over us and took us down to the wardroom to try to clean the oil off us.

We borrowed clothes off the *Haida* crew. When we arrived in Plymouth we were taken to the navy barracks and eventually back home. Glad to be alive!"

Ted Hewitt
V-17860
"B" Gun
October 16, 1921 – December 22, 2001

Ted Hewitt served onboard the *Athabaskan* from the start. In fact, Ted was there while they were still putting the finishing touches on the ship to make her ready for sail. When the workers discovered that Teddy, as he was known to his mates, was a machinist in his life back home in Canada, he was sequestered into such a position on deck. He was put to work machining and welding various plates and turrets to the deck.

Teddy retold countless stories to his son Kim, detailing everyday life on board the ship. When the *Athabaskan* was sent to spend her days in the Arctic at Scapa Flow, he remembered the captain ordering the heat to be turned off. This would commence with the start of their journey from the Azores well up into the frigid waters in preparation for conditioning the men into withstanding the cold temperatures that would face them on a daily basis.

At the same time, they were issued new coats made of wool. The coats, obviously meant to offset the cold, quickly became a dismal failure. The arctic waters splashing constantly over the bow and all the condensation in the air quickly froze to their newly issued coats. So frozen would they become that Teddy recalled how he could lift both feet off the deck, and the stiffened coat would support his weight.

In the event that something was accidentally lost overboard, the routine entailed throwing a weighted buoy overboard to mark the spot where the missing object had gone in. This was used as guidance for the divers who would then retrieve it. On one occasion an anchor was lost. One of the sailors then proceeded to throw the designated marker overboard. Instead of throwing it under the lifelines, he threw it over. However, he couldn't lift the weighted end over with it. Two or three tried together to heave the weight over. Upon seeing the struggle unfold, one of the sailors, being a big, tough Maritimer, yelled "Get outta the way, I'll do it," to which they obediently stepped aside and watched in awe as this great hulk of a man effortlessly tossed the heavy weight over the lifelines.

The Athabaskans had their share of laughter and camaraderie. Teddy recalled one incident that took place at port in Plymouth when a youth was spotted walking along the jetty carrying what appeared to be a liquor bottle. Several of the sailors were hanging over the lifelines having a smoke and watching the events of the day unfold. "Hey lad, what have you got in that bottle?" yelled one of the men. The boy replied that he was just carrying seawater. As the sailors guffawed with one another about what the young lad really had, the same Athabaskan negotiated payment to relieve the lad of his possession.

With the transaction completed, the sailor immediately hid his contraband amongst the belongings in his locker. When the opportunity arose, the sailor fetched his bottle to take a swig. He threw his head back for a taste of the liquid treasure and immediately started to spit, and choke. It seems that the murky substance in the bottle was indeed seawater.

Teddy was the last rescued Athabaskan to be pulled off the cork nets on *Haida's* side. So badly burned was he, that he was almost totally swathed in bandages and taken immediately to a hospital in Basingstoke, England. After two months in hospital Teddy was shipped home to Canada.

His family, not knowing if he was dead or alive, was in for a real shock. Teddy was making his way up the long dusty laneway to the family farmhouse in Woodstock, Ontario. Along the way, he surprised a neighbour lady outside her home. Upon seeing Teddy, not knowing if he was a ghost or real, she dropped what she was doing and started to run up the path ahead of him, yelling at the top of her lungs "Teddy's home, Teddy's home!" His mother was outside her home, weeding the garden. When she straightened up to see what all the commotion was about, she was startled to see her long lost son, Teddy, and fainted to the ground.

Years later, a Legionnaire friend of Teddy's had a chance encounter with a woman by the name of Lily Wilks in a nursing home in his native town of Woodstock. She told Teddy's friend how she had worked in a hospital in Basingstoke, England, as a nurse during the war. While there she had attended many burn victims from a ship's disaster. The friend remembered that Teddy had suffered such a fate and was also a survivor from the sea. He inquired as to whether Lily would like to meet his friend Teddy.

A meeting was arranged, and Lily and Teddy met at the local nursing home. Lily, it turned out, was none other than the nurse on duty that first morning Teddy had been brought into Basingstoke hospital. She had been sent in to feed him breakfast. At the time, Teddy's face was totally wrapped in bandages, except for breathing passages. His eyes had suffered burns as had many of the others, and he was unable to see. The irony to this whole situation is that Lily was now almost totally blind by the time of their second encounter, thus the two old acquaintances were never able to see each other's face.

Lieutenant Leslie Ward
0-76040
1908 – April 29, 1944

Peter Ward, son of Lieutenant Leslie Ward was a young lad of thirteen years when his dad was sent overseas. Leslie was sent to temporarily replace the resident Lieutenant-Commander as head of Canadian Naval Information in London, while Commander Bartlett was on the front lines in Italy. "Mom and I said goodbye to Dad in early April of 1944 at the old downtown Ottawa railway station." Leslie Ward departed St. John's Newfoundland in a corvette escort on its way to Londonderry. On April 26, 1944, Peter's mom received a telegram from Leslie announcing his safe arrival in England, after crossing the Irish Sea and traveling to London via train.

Once in the London office Ward chided the senior officer, whom he knew, about taking off and leaving Ward in London to fill in. The senior officer replied with "if you want a trip, the *Athabaskan* and *Haida* are leaving Plymouth at 2200 this evening and you are welcome to travel aboard one of the ships if you can make it before sailing time."

Ward and his traveling partner, Sub-Lieutenant Jack Mahoney caught the train to Plymouth and raced to the dockyard upon arrival, to keep their date with a destroyer. Ward had inquired as to which ship was the oldest and was told it was *Haida* to which he replied "I'll go on *Athabaskan* then, there will be more room."

Back in Ottawa, Mrs. Ward had taken her son Peter to the Mayfair Theatre on Bank Street to celebrate Leslie's safe arrival in England. Peter recalled "I remember it was a Fred Astair and Ginger Rogers movie." About halfway through the movie his mother suddenly tightened up in her seat and gasped "We have to go home!" "What's wrong?" Peter asked, "the movie's not over yet." She said she didn't know, but she was cold and shaking and so they went home. They were to learn later that her "attack" took place at the exact moment the *Athabaskan* was hit!

Five years later when on a Naval cadet training course on HMCS *Antigonish*, Peter chanced to meet Chief Petty Officer Charles Burgess who was an *Athabaskan* survivor. Burgess recalled the two officers coming onboard ship in Plymouth at the last minute. He remembered seeing the pair up on the after signal deck during the action. That location is almost directly above the site of the first torpedo hit on the port side. Burgess was one of those rescued by *Haida's* cutter.

Photographer Jack Mahoney is buried at Plouescat cemetery. Leslie Ward's body was never recovered.

Stuart Alexander Kettles
V-6748
Leading Writer RCNVR
September 1, 1917 – May 20, 1966

Leading writer Stuart Kettles was a prisoner of war until the camp was liberated in 1945. His many writings have graced several books and documents. The following is a poem written by Stuart as he was held captive.

HMCS ATHABASKAN

There is a little story
That I wish to tell
Of the last time we left Plymouth
For the unknown waiting Hell

It was early in the Springtime
Just a couple of days before
We had returned to our welcome haven
Feeling proud, having boasted our score
We slipped slowly away in the evening
Heading straight for the old French coast
And little was thought that in the morning
T'would be Hitler's turn to boast

The boys never thought or worried
Of the "runs" we were doing of late
But little we knew of this one
Was shrouded and guided by fate

There was no mistaking the orders
"Attack enemy shipping ahead"
So through these cold Channel waters
At thirty-five knots we sped
The enemy shipping was sighted
Destroyers, but that wasn't all
For Crazy and mad a Hitler may seem
He had more than that on the ball

Behind some nearby Islands
Lay E-Boats quite unseen
Which the Radar operator
Could not see upon the screen

The star shell found our target
The Destroyers not far away
And at this Crucial Moment
The E-Boats made their play

From behind their protecting Islands
these E-Boats made their dash
Firing their torpedoes
Which hit us with a crash

Just aft of the torpedo tubes
The first one found its mark
Exploded with a muffled roar
And flames broke through the dark

"X" and "Y" guns were no more
Destroyed just like their crew
The Pom-Pom was a crumpled wreck
And it was also through

Just after the break of morning
The second "fish" hit true
Finding one of the boiler rooms
And immediately it blew

The shower of sparks and shrap that flew
Through the early morning air
Found a resting place in many a man
Told the rest of us "BEWARE"

We crouched in any protected spot
With a prayer upon our lips
And when the din was over
We're forced to leave the ship

Some were badly injured
Others terribly burned
And as we hit the water
Our attention to them was turned

Some wanted to give up the fight
To sleep forever more
We did our best to give them strength
Till we hit the distant shore
They seemed to die all around us
It was pitiful to see
How can others calmly say
"Tis the price of VICTORY"

A few got back to England
About forty-six in all
While those who hadn't perished
Went behind the Atlantic Wall

Now we are the "gefangeners"
In a German prison camp
And as we think of loved ones
Sometimes our eyes are damp

We feel that in the battle
His life our skipper lost
A finer man I never knew
It was a hellish cost

So please do not forget those boys
Who dressed in NAVY BLUE
And fought on the "ATHABASKAN"
And gave their all for you

Kettles described his departure from the ship in the early morning hours of April 29 in his log:

> "I looked over the side at that cold uninviting water of the English Channel by now covered with thick, dirty, fuel oil. My first thought was 'Gee, I can't jump into that, ' but when I turned around and looked at the burning ship, which was beginning to settle to her watery grave, I suddenly decided, 'Hell, I can't stay here neither.' There was no shock when you hit the water, but it wasn't very doggone long until we soon realized that it was no Turkish Bath."

Haida came into view to collect survivors. He recounted in his diary:

> I started to swim to the directed place. I just had about twelve more feet to go when the *Haida* threw her engines into reverse, the force of the water from her propellers washed me away from her side out about a quarter mile from the bow. I now found myself entirely alone, and my legs and arms were growing numb as the minutes passed. The tide which was going out at the time, came in long slow rolling waves. This caused a very nice sensation, like rocking a child to sleep in a cradle, and it wasn't long before this motion began to make me very sleepy. There were none of the other lads around to talk to, to stay awake. I felt myself going to sleep, and knowing I couldn't stay awake much longer, pulled up the head rest on my life jacket and was quite prepared to take whatever lay ahead of me, even though I should fall asleep, which is exactly what happened.
>
> The next time I saw the welcome rays of sun was quite different. I lay on a wooden table, naked as the day I was born, shivering from the cold immersion. I asked where we were, the answer "On a German Destroyer."
>
> Upon being sent to the prison camp in northern Germany, Stuart and some of the others were immediately placed into solitary confinement. He slept on a wooden bunk with a straw mattress covered in rough material similar to a potato sack and was given two meager blankets. He cited that the Germans finally decided to give them toothpaste and a brush after three and a half weeks.
>
> For twenty-eight days, the meal menu was the same. Breakfast was comprised of two slices of black bread with no margarine or jam, and a cup of ersatz tea. Lunch was a small bowl of soup with three to four potatoes in their skins, and supper was the same as breakfast.
>
> Three times daily, come rain, snow, or sleet, the inmates were mustered for count in the courtyard. An electrically operated radio, smuggled in by a couple of sympathetic guards kept them up-to-date on the war effort.

Stuart recalled other interesting segments of daily life in the camp with: "In the early days of our captivity, ferocious, trained police dogs were employed to guard the prisoners," but by judicious, surreptitious use of food and petting, their ferocity melted away. One day the German guards entering the barracks were shocked to find several of their man-eating dogs lying under the bunks with the men, licking their faces. The guards promptly posted a notice in English that the dogs were absolutely forbidden to accept food from the prisoners.

As Germany's manpower dwindled, younger guards were sent off to the front lines of the army and replaced with the aging veterans of 1918. When food packages for seamen arrived at the village three miles distant, a detail of POWs was sent under these guards to bring them in. The walk frequently proved too strenuous for the decrepit jailers and the seamen would carry their rifles for them and give them lifts in the carts. Before arriving back at camp they would help the guards from the carts, button their tunics, smarten them up and generally hand back their rifles to make sure they would not be replaced by "younger, hard-boiled guards."

Robert Dalzell
4141
January 13, 1921 – August 5, 2003

The following excerpts are taken from the wartime diary of Robert Dalzell, Prisoner of War

The Sinking of H.M.C.S. *Athabaskan*
on the 29th of April 1944

"The H.M.C.S. *Athabaskan* was a destroyer of the Tribal class commissioned on February 3rd, 1943 and until she sank, had a colourful history which can be found in my diary."

Friday, April 28, 1944 they set sail out of Plymouth for mine laying operations off the coast of Normandy. Everything was quiet until they received a signal on their radar showing two echoes.

"This signal was received at 3:45 a.m on the 29th of April. We sped up to thirty knots in a N.E. direction going towards the Cherbourg Peninsula. We detected the two echoes on our 276 Radar set almost immediately. Orders came through from the bridge to me to switch on the 285 Radar Gunnery Set. My first ranges of the enemy were 12 thousand yards and six thousand yards at Red 20 off the port bow. I told the bridge of the distance of the three echoes, two at 12 tho, and 1 at 6.

They ordered me to range on the farther one at 12 tho. yards."

Dalzell kept sending continuous ranges and when the enemy was about six thousand yards away, they heard a tremendous explosion that was coming from the stern of the ship. The explosion knocked out his sextant.

Fire erupted from the explosion, knocking out the after gun turrets and the multi pom poms. "The firing gear and motive power of the ship was blown to hell, namely the propellers and their shafts and the hydraulic steering motors.

"The blast blew a depth-charge, weighing app. 500 to 700 pounds, from the rails on the very stern of the ship, over top of the entire ship, and it landed on the barrels of "A" gun on the forecastle." This all took place in just a few seconds, then "B" Gun turret recommenced to fire in a couple of minutes after the hit.

All the while, the burning ship was drifting with the tide and illuminating the skies, making them a "perfect target for the enemy."

"The order came from the bridge to go and stand by our abandon ship station. "B" gun had only fired a couple of salvos after the hit. We shut the 285 set partly off and came out of the office on the flag deck and went around on the starboard side and into the chart room under the bridge aft of the wheelhouse. The Captain Lt. Cdr. Stubbs D.S.O. was there gathering up an armful of confidential codebooks. He spoke to me and said 'Dalzell, you had better go to your abandon ship station.'

"I came out of the chart room and had a hazy idea the Captain was behind me, and went out on the flag deck on the starboard side. The pom pom ammo was exploding and making a terrific noise. The flames were shooting up in the heavens and it seemed as if all hell was turned loose. Some of the hands could be seen trying to connect up hoses but it weren't going to be very successful."

Dalzell went from the fly deck down to the break of the forecastle. Just as he was about to proceed down to the upper deck, there was a terrific flash and a scorching blast of hot air hit him and knocked him down on the deck, with his left side facing aft.

"After the flames died down I struggled to my feet to find I was minus my pants and one of my oxfords. My body seemed to be on fire. I looked about me and could see no one because my eyes had burned temporarily blinded by the flash. I could hear a number of voices screaming in agony. I went down the ladder to the upper deck and made my way to the guardrail and scrambled over. By this time I could see a few feet in front of me and I jumped out from the ship and grabbed the whaler's forward fall and slid down till I was in the partly submerged whaler.

"When scrambling out of the whaler I found the water very, very cold after the terrific heat of the flames. I swam away from the ship and stopped just once to look back and saw the bow pointing towards the sky and then swam as hard as possible so that I wouldn't be pulled under by the suction. Looking back again in a few minutes I couldn't see nothing whatever of the ship. I could hear the other destroyer that was accompanying us still firing away at the enemy. This also was a Tribal, H.M.C.S. *Haida*.

"I could hear voices all about me in the water. Some raised in panic and others shouting instructions as to what to do, and what not to do. I was a little unconcerned with this as I was trying to locate a float. Finally, after about ten minutes I got alongside one and found Lt. Comm. Lantier and about twenty-five others hanging on."

After ten minutes or so, someone shouted that the *Haida* was coming. The less injured made an effort to swim to her. Dalzell felt like he was in a dreamlike state. His vision was very bad because of his burns. The *Haida* maneuvered slowly among the men and lowered her motorboat to pick up some of the boys.

"After the *Haida* left, I took Ed McCloy [from Brockville, Ont] who was hanging onto the back of my life jacket and started out to look for another float as the one we were on was very overcrowded. We managed to reach another float and then I blacked out.

"The next thing I remember I was being hauled aboard a German motorboat. Then we headed for France which was only a few miles away. I came to on the jetty and I had been stripped of my life jacket. We were then marched through the streets of the village and taken into a courtyard."

By ten in the morning, Dalzell was in a lot of pain. The skin was hanging in shreds from his hands, face and legs. The survivors were left until about two in the afternoon without medical aid. A large bus finally arrived with German guards, and took them to Brest, about twenty miles away. Upon arrival in Brest, they were taken to the German naval barracks and given first aid. Then, ambulances were sent to transport the injured to hospital.

They remained in Brest till the ninth of May when they were taken by ambulances from the hospital to the railway station and loaded into a hospital coach. They journeyed for two days, finally arriving in Orleans on May 11th, where they were taken to a prisoner of war hospital. The staff at the hospital were all French. They remained at the French hospital until the 15th of June. When they left there to be moved to Germany, they were forced to leave five of their fellow prisoners behind.

While en route to Germany, they witnessed a great deal of damage which had been caused by the bombing. Upon their arrival on June 18th, they were placed in cells where they were to remain for nine days.

"Then I was shifted to another cell but one that afforded a few more privileges. Here I received a Red Cross parcel of which I had not had

Prison Camp. (courtesy Ron Reynolds)

one since three weeks before we left Orleans. I stayed two weeks in this cell and then I was allowed to move into the next compound where we were all together. We remained here for three weeks, then on a Monday we were moved down to Marlag (N) which was about five minutes walk from Dulag. On Tuesday, the day following my arrival, I was leaving on the train at three in the morning.

"I left at three on Wednesday morning and I was taken to Frankfurt and then to a cell outside the city. Here I remained for three days being questioned by the Gestapo. Then I was sent to an air force transit camp where I remained four days. I left there and returned to Marlag but had to spend the night in an air raid shelter in Bremen, going the next morning the last 25 miles to Milag N."

William Stewart, on right, with Hamilton pal William Connolly.

William G. Stewart
V-8866
Signalman
December 10, 1921 – April 29, 1944

Bill grew up with the talent and propensity for art. The popular, athletic young man was the eldest of five boys. He enrolled in the signal school at St. Hyacinthe, Quebec where he excelled and graduated at the top of his class. His artistic talent was put to good use when he designed the insignia for the HMCS *Athabaskan*, depicting an Indian warrior sitting astride a rearing pinto pony, wearing the face-paint of war. His model was none other than his close Hamilton buddy, Bill Connolly.

On April 30, 1944, the morning after the ship sank, the Stewart family were having breakfast when the news came over the CBC radio. They listened intently as the announcer spoke of the ship sinking in the Channel. Mrs. Stewart cried out "My son has gone!" Across the country from coast to coast, many *Athabaskan* mothers were having the same reaction.

The previous night in the Stewart household, Bill's dad had been awakened from his sleep in the middle of the night upon hearing the front door of the house open. Mr. Stewart listened intently as he heard footsteps slowly climb the stairs, walk down the hall and one by one stop at each bedroom door. When his bedroom door opened, he sat bolt upright in his bed. He was startled to see a shirtless Bill standing at the foot of his bed, covered in oil. No words were spoken and a few moments later he disappeared as quickly as he had appeared. At that moment Mr. Stewart knew that Bill was dead!

(1)

Observing the trad-
itional Christmas
routine the youngest
member of the ship's
company becomes C.O.
for the day.Athabaskan
did not overlook this
rule-there was much
confusion as this O/D'S
sympathies laywith
the lower deck rates,
consiquently there were
a number of officers
who stopped a blast
from this stroppy
seaman...

What have we here?
Ah, yes, this beautiful
hunk of man, believe
it or not,started the
day with full intentions
of staying in the rig
but it seems that a
Gremlin stepped in
and slipped him a
Mickie. As the alcohol
made Borris feel
quite warm he began
to disrobe but
fortunately this is as far
as he got....

(2)

Christmas dinnerwas
an interesting event
for us this year.
The one and only
Connolly took it upon
himself to carve the
turkey, which inciden-
-tally wasn't really
as tough as the
illustration shows,
but he sure did wade
right into that bird.
There was a good deal
of cussing coming from
the head of the mess
table but finally we
all put on the feed bag,
tucked the ears back
and dug out...

It's odd in the Navy
to have the leading
hand of a mess to
dish up after the
mad scramble of gannets.
This being a special
occasion though it
was the case.They
kinda' took the strain
as we had a few Sigs
and Coders from a
Juicer ship as guests.
The killicks didn't
seem to mind as every-
-one had the Xmas
spirit (5 pts. of beer)...

(3)

Christmas day itself
was spent out on that
green rolling stuff
but this handicap didn't
prevent us from exchang-
-ing small gifts. They
weren't much actually
but it did help us to
remember that the folks
at home were doing the
same thing.- Joe said
he wanted to get rid
of the sweater his
gal sent anyway...

Some folk are under
the impression that
lockers are a stowage
place for gear only-
not a bit. One of
their many uses is for tired ratings who
are toolazy to sling their carts and prefer
to recline on top of these lockers.
Scanlon, who is now
growing a beard,
(it says here)

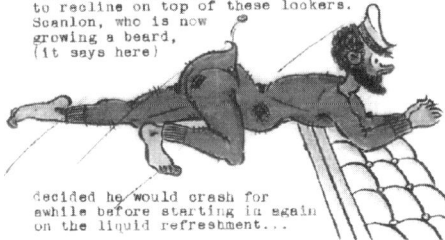

decided he would crash for
awhile before starting in again
on the liquid refreshment...

Christmas mail was not
brought aboard until we
arrived at our home port
during the latter part of
December. The mailman
thought he was having a
nitemare when 119 bags-
(don't get me wrong0,were
waiting to be sorted and
distributed but some of
the boys gave a very
willing helping hand.

William Stewart's Christmas Letter Home - December, 1943. (courtesy Ed Stewart)

When the war was over, a signalman friend of Bill's arrived at the Stewart family home to talk about Bill's passing, as they had been the closest of friends. Bill's friend revealed that the last time he saw Bill alive, they were standing at the side of the ship together ready to jump overboard. And indeed Bill was shirtless as his shirt had been blown off in the blast!

Harry Hurwitz
V-31067
Able Seaman
B Gun
October 1, 1921

Born into a Montreal, Quebec household, Harry was one of thirteen children. Six boys joined the service, two of whom were in the navy during the war, while one sister joined the WACs. Harry was an Athabaskan crewmember from commissioning day to the end. Harry recalled the night shifts at sea as a crewmember of "B" guns, four hours on duty and four hours off. They would be served hot cocoa frequently during their shifts to help keep them awake. After one such night shift, Harry returned to his cabin exhausted and flopped into his hammock for his long anticipated shut-eye. Seems as if Ginger the cat had beaten him to it. Always looking for a prank to pull for laughs, some of Harry's cohorts had placed Ginger there to surprise him. Ginger had a rude awakening when Harry collapsed into the hammock. He fell onto the unsuspecting cat, which proceeded to scratch and claw her way out from under a startled Harry. Literally the fur flew! Amidst much screaming and wailing from both Harry and the cat, the two extricated themselves from the hammock, Harry flying in one direction and the terrified cat in another. To this day Harry hates cats.

After the first torpedo struck the *Athabaskan* on the 29th of April, Harry on "B" gun was sent to get a hose from amidship to help extinguish the raging fires. He was turned back by the intense heat and flames. That surely saved his

PRISONER OF WAR PARCEL COLIS DE PRISONNIER DE GUERRE KRIEGSGEFANGENENSENDUNG		POSTAGE FREE FRANC DE PORT GEBUHRENFREI		
SERIAL NO. X9/4/X 79432 TOBACCO PRODUCTS MANUFACTURED BY: IMPERIAL TOBACCO COMPANY OF CANADA, LIMITED, MONTREAL. - CANADA		LIST OF CONTENTS SENDER MUST ITEMIZE	NET WEIGHT LBS. OZS.	VALUE $ c
SENDER: ENVOYEUR: ABSENDER: MRS. H. HURWITT, 6093 PARK AVE., MONTREAL, P.Q. CANADA CANADA		300 SWEET CAP. CIGARETTES	12	7
ADDRESSED TO: ADRESSÉ À: RANK AND NAME A/S. HARRY HURWITT, PRISONER OF WAR NO. 1306 CAMP: LAGER BEZEICHUNG, MARLAG UND MILAG NORD (MILAG),		ADRESSIERT AN: *MA* GERMANY		

Parcel label from home. (courtesy Harry Hurwitz)

life, for the second explosion occurred where he had been heading. By the time the captain gave the orders to abandon ship, Harry had stripped his heavy boots and coat off, not wanting to be weighed down in the water. At the time he jumped from the rising ship's bow into the cold Atlantic waters, he was wearing only a t-shirt, pants and his socks. "It seemed like seven or eight seconds of falling through the air before I finally hit the water from the height I jumped. My whole life flashed before my eyes. I saw my mother and father and all my brothers and sisters."

Harry remembered being told to swim as far away from the ship as he could get because the suction from the sinking ship might pull him down with it. He swam like crazy to put as much distance as he could between himself and the sinking ship. With all the floating debris about, he was able to latch onto a piece of the masthead. Another sailor had already beaten him to the makeshift float. When he asked the other seaman, all covered in oil, "who are you?" the reply came: "Stubbs."

With that, Harry replied, "Oh, Captain Stubbs." "No," said the captain, "just call me John." Protocol dictates that under their circumstance, when all sailors are in the water, there is no rank among the crew. All men are then equal.

After what seemed like hours, Harry saw a carley float drifting by, empty. He swam over and climbed inside. Others followed suit until there were ten or twelve men in their new-found safe haven. Eventually, in the daylight hours following the sinking, a large German heavy cruiser picked them up and took them to shore.

They were greeted at the jetty by a number of SS Gestapo and made to march down the gangplank with their hands up. Each sailor was interrogated individually. Harry was very concerned because he was the only Jewish captive brought ashore. When the interrogator inquired as to how to spell his name, Harry cleverly dropped the "Z" from his surname. He was asked where his parents were born. Harry responded by telling the questioning SS officer that they were both born in London, England. In actual fact, his

Sketch from war diary of Harry Hurwitz.

father was born in Russia and his mother in Latvia. As the inquisition progressed, the SS officer started to laugh when Harry told him where he was born. When Harry inquired as to what was so funny, the SS responded with "I worked for General Electric in Lachine, Quebec for a few years prior to the war." It seems the officer had immigrated to Canada after serving in WWI. At the onset of WWII, the German returned to his motherland to "fight the Russians."

After his lengthy train ride into Germany, followed by another long ride in the back of a big truck to the prison camp, Harry was fingerprinted and given the prison number 1306.

In camp, Harry kept a logbook. It was filled with writings, poems, and sketches rendered by some of the other inmates. Like the other prisoners, he looked forward to receiving his Red Cross parcels. The food consumed by the prisoners, consisted of their Red Cross stipends and

what they could get from trading cigarettes to the Germans for potatoes, vegetables or whatever else they could glean. Each cabin was supplied with twelve bricks of coal to fuel their potbellied stove.

"I remember the Red Cross parcels well," said Harry. "They consisted of a container of coffee, two pieces of hardtack, a small tin of powdered milk, sardines, a tin of salmon, and a little packet of raisins, plus of course cigarettes. Tuesdays were farmer's market days where you could trade three or four cigarettes for a local chicken."

Once, the German officers were preparing for a dance to be held on a Saturday night. They had their food all lined up, but lacked coffee. Knowing that the sailors had coffee in their food parcels, the Germans bartered for a tin of real coffee in exchange for a bushel of apples. The deal was struck and the sailors were salivating just thinking about sinking their teeth into the promised apples. It wasn't long before the men realized they didn't have a whole container of coffee to fulfill their portion of the bargain. But it was wartime, what could they do? Not to let such a minor obstacle stand in the way of their promised treasure, someone came up with an alternate solution.

It came as quite a surprise when the German merrymakers went to make the coffee on their festive evening. As they removed the lid, they discovered to their chagrin that beneath the top layer of coffee in the tin, was nothing but dirt! A day later, one officer yelling at the sailors in his broken English, was heard to say, "You think you so smart, you think you pull wool over our eyes. We get even with you!"

The following are two short poems taken from Harry's diary.

Prisoner Of War
Barbed wire all around us
Clothing full of lice
Chunks of cheese for breakfast
For tea a mug of rice.

A Prisoner of War's Grace
Dry bread - No meat
Please God - Let's eat
Amen

One day at camp, a hole in the fence was spotted by some of the inmates. Harry and a couple of other prisoners decided to make a run for it. After taking a look around to see if anyone was watching, they slipped through the hole in the fence and walked away from camp. After scurrying up the dusty road for a half hour, dressed in old army jackets (so as not to get shot at), the men decided they were thirsty. Out on the horizon appeared a large farmhouse to where they made their way.

When they knocked at the front door, an elderly woman appeared and led them into her living room. Because of the similarities between the German and Yiddish languages, Harry spoke to the woman in Yiddish and asked for a drink of water. They sat patiently waiting while the woman shuffled off to the kitchen to fulfill their request. While in the other room, out of earshot, the woman proceeded to crank up the telephone and call the local authorities to tell them she had some escaped prisoners sitting in her living room.

Moments later, three trucks and four motorcycles with twenty soldiers screeched to a halt amidst the swirling cloud of dust in her yard. Orders were shouted to the escapees to "come out with your hands up!" The prisoners waving a white bed sheet appeared on the porch and were immediately evacuated to a waiting truck. They were searched and thrown into jail until the camp officer had them released and returned to their barbed-wire yard. Freedom was short but sweet while it lasted.

Explosion as rendered in diary of Harry Hurwitz.

As liberation approached, an advance tank from the Scots brigade was sent to tell the prisoners not to leave the camp before the full force arrived to set them free because "we shoot and ask questions later." On April 29, 1945, at 6:00 a.m., one year to the day after their ship had sunk in the Atlantic, the Scots Brigade arrived. Switches to the electricity were turned off and the tanks mowed down the fences of the prison yard. Harry recalled all the inmates hugging and kissing their liberators.

The following poem was taken from the pages of Harry Hurwitz' wartime diary. It is the result of collaboration between him and the fellow prisoners from his cabin.

My Canada
Canada my Canada, my soul and my life
Your heart beats for us in joy or in strife
You gave me Dear Canada a bed and a home
To return to no matter when I chanced a roam
In poverty or wealth, on land or on sea,
Winning or losing my heart beats for thee
Though understanding of favours
There's one thing I crave
When I die My Dear Canada
May your earth be my grave.

Samuel M. Fillatre
A-5043
Able Seaman
June 7, 1918 – October 29, 1969

Samuel Fillatre, a twenty-five-year-old Nova Scotia native, noted in his war diary "on the morning of the 26th (3 - 4 a.m.) we engage three enemy destroyers and score hits on them all.

One we set afire and finally sink, another we drive ashore. Our total casualties are one killed at his gun position of HMCS *Huron*."

On Friday, April 28th, 1944 at 0200 hours Fillatre records the "Last Action."

"Receive signal from shore wireless station ordering us to intercept enemy convoy proceeding along the coast of France. Cease mine laying and 'Rev' up to intercept." At 0345 hours he notes "Sight three enemy destroyers and prepare for action – close in." At 0400 hours: "First salvoes from enemy destroyers fall short, landing astern. We open with all 4.7's and maneuver for position."

At 0410 Fillatre is aware of the ship being hit aft. "These hits render "X and Y" guns out of action and blowing up the "Pom Pom" fire breaks out from the magazines enveloping the stern in a mess of flames and explosions are frequent. Our engines are rendered useless and the ship comes to a stop, slowly settling by the stern. "A" gun resumes firing."

0420. "Order from the bridge passed by word of mouth, to prepare to abandon ship. Magazine crews and engine room branch secure their positions and proceed to their abandon ship stations. Gun crews abandon their now useless guns, and endeavour to secure towlines to *Haida*."

At 0425 he reports the second torpedo hit at the break of the foc'sle where fires erupt yet again from the burst oil drums and tanks all along the starboard side. The ship lists to port and "Abandon Ship" is now the general order.

By 0430, the ship is settling rapidly with the bow slowly standing clear of the water. Two motor cutters, the whaler and nine out of ten carley floats are now useless. At this point Fillatre escapes the fiery inferno over the starboard side and swims strongly away from the ship.

His last sight of the dying warrior was "of the bow as she slides down into the depths of the English Channel." Like the other sailors, he too describes the "oily" water, the cold and unrecognizable faces of his mates. They all watch as starshells fired by *Haida* and the enemy destroyers fill the early morning sky, with their sister ship breaking away from the action to steam slowly towards the littered surface of the sea to pick up survivors.

Fillatre's rescue was at the hands of the Germans who appeared on the horizon at daybreak with two minesweepers and two auxiliary ships, presumably air/sea rescue vessels.

"Enemy ships heave to and proceed to pick up survivors, and none too soon as everyone is suffering from exposure and quite a few have gone under as a result of burns and the temperature of the water."

En route to the port of Brest, France, the enemy rescuers "man their guns to ward off attacking RAF bomber aircraft." This unsettling experience was described by Fillatre as "After our nerves, such as they are left of them, have settled down to normal, the paravanes encounter and explode one of our mines. We arrive in Brest, the old rendezvous of the *Scharnhorst*. Over the gangway in single file, we are photographed by German newsreel cameramen." They are loaded into trucks and given a "conducted tour of the city of Brest."

Arriving at the camps, Marlag and Milag Nord, which hold about eight hundred prisoners, "we are marched into the theatre and pass single file by long rows of tables. On these tables we put what little clothing and gear we possess, the Germans then proceed to search it."

Their new accommodation consists of ten large rooms in a hut, eight of which house fourteen men and two rooms hold two men. Each room features a stove for cooking, "crude but efficient."

The next day they assemble and march up to another larger building to get their prisoner-of-war numbers. Fillatre's statement of resignation says it all. "Here's where we are and here's what we have become. Now officially we are *Gefangenen*."

Douglas & Ingar
Laurie on their
wedding day
April 21, 1943.
(courtesy of D.
Laurie)

Ingar Marie Laurie
(nee Hansen)
February 24, 1918

Ingar was from Greenock, a little Scottish town nestled on the Firth of Clyde. As a port town, it was subjected to Axis bombings. Sometimes the bombing continued incessantly from morning till night. On one such occasion, the Hansen family was awakened around 11:00 p.m. when the fury of the bombs decimated their neighbourhood, including their own home. Ingar's brother-in-law was killed carrying his daughter to safety. He was trying to protect her with his body when he was hit.

While *Athabaskan* frequently appeared at the town of Greenock, on that particular night she was out at sea on a mission. Ingar recalls the crew later being ordered onshore to help clean up the debris from the destruction. The young sailors scrambled ashore to assist however they could in the aftermath of the attack.

On a sunny day in 1941, Ingar was walking along the street in Greenock with her girlfriend Janey, when two handsome sailors tried to strike up a conversation with them. The girls, feigning indifference, kept on walking. As the young gentlemen continued to follow and chat, they asked for directions to their destination. The girls responded with, "Well, you're heading in the right direction," and kept on walking.

Life during wartime was surreal and was taking the two friends in different directions. Ingar and Janey did not see one another for several months until Ingar received an invitation to attend Janey's wedding. And who should the groom be but Harry, one of the two sailors seeking the favour of two lovely Scottish women of some months prior. The best man was Douglas Laurie, the other of the two Canadian sailors. Douglas and Ingar spent some time together with friends and getting to know one another and finally their acquaintance turned into dating.

Ingar was heading to England for a job outside London. Laurie was also going to England, as he was waiting for his "calling up papers" to the new Canadian Tribal, *Athabaskan*.

The young sailor showed up to escort Ingar to the train station, bound for London. He proposed to his young Scottish sweetheart there, on the spot, in the station. They were married in St. Johns Anglican Church, in Greenock, Scotland on April 21, 1943 a few months later.

Not long after their wedding, Laurie put to sea on the *Athabaskan* from Newcastle, England. After the glider-bomb attack, *Athabaskan* was again in port in Greenock for repairs. Laurie, nursing a back injury from the hit, was on leave while the ship was in for refit. With Laurie back at sea again on a newly overhauled vessel, Ingar left for Canada on board the *Ile de France*, in an evacuation of war brides.

Crossing the Atlantic was rough but Ingar made friends with some other war brides, also making their way to their new homes in Canada, and the time passed quickly for the young women. The *Ile de France* landed in Montreal and Ingar proceeded to Elrose, Saskatchewan by train to stay with Laurie's family.

A month later, Ingar left for Victoria, B.C. and headed north to stay with her old friend Janey, also a war bride, now living in Port Alberni. Early one morning Ingar witnessed Janie answer the door, receive a telegram, and quickly hide it in a drawer. The telegram, addressed to Ingar, announced the ship's sinking.

First word home of his fate. (courtesy D. Laurie)

Shortly thereafter, Ingar left to stay with another friend from her hometown of Greenock. Maryanne was now living with her in-laws in Westminster, B.C., where her father-in-law was the head warden of Oakalla Prison. It was here she received her first word from Laurie, with the postcard stating he was interred at a prison camp in Germany.

After the war, Ingar traveled by train back to Saskatoon for the long anticipated return of her husband from his internment. With the war behind them, Ingar and Douglas Laurie set up their home in Victoria, to raise their children, and at this writing, celebrated sixty-six years of marriage.

Douglas T. L. Laurie
21532
Chief Stoker Petty Officer
March 5, 1919

Doug Laurie, a young Saskatechewan man, boarded the *Athabaskan* as a newly married sailor with the Scottish bride he'd met while awaiting his call to duty aboard the Tribal. One year later his ship sank beneath him in the chilly Atlantic waters.

"I remember we were always on watch and on damage control. We always wore life jackets. My action station was at the aft end. At the time of the hit, I was in Boiler Room No.2 and came up on deck and stayed on deck as long as I could. When the ship started to roll, I knew I had to jump."

He jumped from the starboard side, and like many other sailors, knew he had to put distance between himself and the ship. Laurie was afraid of being caught not only by the suction but also by the numerous wires that held the threat of entanglement.

"There were several comrades around me in the water, at a distance. I remember talking to a friend, Edward Beaver. I kept talking to him and then realized he wasn't answering...he was gone." At 4:00 in the morning, he recalled it being very cold. He floated with about twenty crewmates on an overcrowded float until he found his own piece of flotsam. *Haida* came into view and he was trying hard to swim and reach it. In the distance, *Haida's* crew were waving at him and yelling words of encouragement to keep swimming. So exhausted was he that he passed out and when he came to and looked around, *Haida* had disappeared.

His rescue arrived with the German ships sent out to pick up the remainder of the survivors. After being hauled out of the water he said "The Germans as I recall had a big knife and cut the clothes and the life jackets right off us." The captors then clothed the men, detained them, and then boarded them onto an overcrowded train for their three-day trip to the prison camp.

Once in the prison, each captive was given clothes provided for them by the Red Cross. When the provisions arrived once a week from the humanitarian service, "The Germans would go through the boxes and take what they wanted. I remember only getting soup from the Germans and a slice of bread. We lived on what the Red Cross gave us. This is when I started smoking as the guys told me I wouldn't be hungry if I smoked. We would trade cigarettes for food from the Germans."

The layout of the camp was in the configuration of a square with towers at each corner, manned by a machine-gun wielding German guard at each outlook. "If we went out of a certain area, they would shoot. This area was called 'no mans land.' During the day we did nothing, just walked about and sometimes played ball. We would watch the planes overhead going by and dropping bombs."

Boredom caused arguing and bickering amongst the inmates about anything and everything and "whatever came up." Their letters home were all censored and this prevented the men from being able to put much information in them. The Germans counted the prisoners three or four times a day, "They would count to make sure we were all there."

Beds in the huts were filled with sawdust and there were no pillows. The inmates discarded their beds and slept on a thin pad. Radios were available because the English prisoners would trade cigarettes for them. "The Germans were easy to bribe." News was shared with the Canadians from the hidden radios the English had stowed away.

Laurie felt the Canadian men were allowed outside the camp on walks because of their nationality. They were treated better than the other prisoners because the Germans had been treated well in Canada, "and so gave us a few extra privileges." On their walkabouts outside the confines of camp, the young men saw many dead Germans lying on the ground who had been killed by the advancing Allies.

Upon their liberation from the prison camp, "The British came and asked which Germans were the 'mean ones'?" The men would point to the designated Germans who they thought were the "mean ones," and these were taken out of the camp by the British. Shots could be heard moments later.

Orders were given by the British not to leave the camp so they would not run the risk of being shot. When the time finally arrived to evacuate the camp, those who had been there the longest, went first. With fresh khaki uniforms provided by the Red Cross, their long incarceration came to an end with a flight back to England and finally a ship home to Canada.

Jean F.A. (Andre) Audet
V-35565
Gunner
March 10, 1922 – December 9, 2008

Andre Audet grew up on a tobacco farm at St. Cesaire, Quebec, as the only son in a farming family which included six daughters. He recalled his father being extremely upset about his joining the navy. His father tried everything he could think of to stop his signing on, including trying to persuade the officers into rejecting Andre's enlistment.

After his initial training in Halifax, he was shipped out on the corvette *Napanee*, then the *Amherst*. From the *Amherst* he was sent to the British HMS *Montgomery* as a rating. Finally, Andre was sent to be a crewmember on the HMCS *Athabaskan*. His trade of machinist came in handy as a shell loader for "B" guns. He recalled living in barracks on shore in England while the *Athabaskan* was getting her finishing touches. Ordinary duties onboard also entailed swabbing the decks and painting the ship when necessary, and of course Mess cleanup.

While living onshore he never saw the bombing of London or neighbouring areas firsthand, but frequently heard the buzz of the bombs. "We got used to them. We just watched them." When on shore leave they frequently stayed at the local YMCA or the Knights of Columbus hall.

On several occasions, the *Athabaskan* retrieved German survivors from the ocean after their ships had been sunk. When they had to bury a sailor at sea, friend or foe,

Andre recalled the procedure. "You put 2 shells in a canvas, wrap them up and the captain would…with the plank, and say a prayer and just slide them in feet first. We did that quite often. And even if they were Germans, you still had to respect them, you know. But when you see your own Canadians, you can't even take them home. You had to bury them at sea. It's really something you know, your friends and all that."

Every day the sailors, twenty-one and older, were issued a ration of rum. To monitor this routine, the chief petty officer served up the rum from a container and watched as you drank it in front of him. This prevented the underage crew from obtaining the liquor.

The day the German destroyer *Scharnhorst* was sunk, *Athabaskan* was quite a distance away. According to Audet they listened to the battle commentary over the PA system. During a 2001 interview, when asked if they were pleased with that, he replied: "Yeah, but you always said a prayer. The captain would muster all the boys together and they would come down in the sun in the morning and we would remember them."

As *Athabaskan* was going to her grave, Audet recalled that "B" guns were still firing away as the ship was sinking lower and lower into the water. He jumped overboard with his crewmate Miller and was eventually picked up by *Haida's* cutter.

On being asked about his return trip to Penzance in the cutter and being "strafed" by the enemy he replied: "Heading to port, heard the noise of 2 planes. Came down to us, saw the swastika so we jumped overboard. One went this way, and one that way and one turned back. Thought we were going to be machine-gunned. And they just came like this, V sign for victory with their fingers. We could see them, just like I see your face now. So close to us and so close to the water. They never fired a shot!"

Joseph (Jim) W. L'Esperance
V-9580
Leading Seaman
October 3, 1917 – May 18, 1988

Twenty-seven-year-old Jim L'Esperance had good cause to fight for his own survival in the cold North Atlantic ocean. Waiting for his safe return home was his wife and two young children, one of whom he had yet to meet. His son was two years old and his baby daughter had been born after he went to sea.

In the cold and dark of the early morning hours, L'Esperance managed to swim to *Haida's* side. A sailor on the scramble net tried desperately to pull him to safety but it was not to be. *Haida* was drifting further and further away from him. He managed to touch fingers to the helping hand extended to pull him on board, but the rescuer was unable to grab his hand. With a sinking heart he could only watch with despair as the ship picked up speed and left him behind.

L'Esperance managed to pull himself onto a piece of floating debris. He could hear someone yelling but in the blackness of the night was unable to see where his mate was. He ventured back into the water to pull someone to the safety of his float. The man was so burned, L'Esperance noted that the man's skin was falling off his hands and face.

The crew of the German ship that plucked L'Esperance from the water offered their ship-full of *Athabaskans* soap to wash with. The cold sailors had stripped their filthy, wet clothes off but try as they may, the soap was unable to wash the oil from their bodies. This particular German vessel had no clothes or blankets to wrap around their captives, so the

Athabaskans had to disembark and march in to the port town of L'Aber Wrac'h naked. L'Esperance recalled being threatened with being shot if they tried to escape.

As prisoner-of-war, he recalled being issued adequate clothing; however, there was no heat or hot water in his part of the compound. The sailors slept in their clothes. Hunger was part of their daily lives as there was never enough food to eat.

L'Esperance was one of the three brave Athabaskans who escaped the prison camp as the remainder were preparing for their long march to another camp. With his freedom he remembered walking down a road and seeing Germany's now useless currency lying in the ditches and littering the roads. It was of no use to anyone now.

On his return home after the war, Jim L'Esperance's wife, three-year-old son Jim and two-year-old daughter Sharon were at the station to greet him. Sharon L'Esperance, Jim's daughter, remembers it being cold and crowded at the station that day waiting for the train to stop and to meet her father for the very first time.

Paul G. Gallant
A-1889
Able Seaman
May 4, 1915 – September 21, 1977

The YMCA issued logbooks to the prisoners-of-war. Some sketched in their books and some, like *Athabaskan* crewman Paul Gallant kept regular entries which helped the prisoner maintain his sanity and, in years down the road, revealed the daily life amid the true hardships endured by the prisoners. The following are stories and excerpts from Gallant's logbook.

Action: Glider Bomb Attack, August 27, 1943

"When I got down to the magazine I wasn't long getting the ammunition on the way to the Guns crew. Soon I heard the 4.7 go and then "X" gun. I knew they were getting in close. Soon all the close range weapons opened up. A few seconds later there was a great explosion and I shut my eyes and held the shell I had in my arms because I expected to see everything go up and all of us with it but nothing happened."

After the ship was rocked a second time Gallant was ordered to "B" guns by the Gunnery Officer where he helped to extinguish the fire caused by the bomb. As he turned about he saw the grisly sight of two shipmates lying dead on the deck, one with a five inch hole in his stomach. Two other injured men walked to sick bay only to die later and the fifth sailor was blown off the ship, never to be seen again.

Egret, a ship traveling in their flotilla was sunk by the Germans during this same action. According to Gallant, *Egret* went down in forty seconds, taking one hundred and eighty-three out of a crew of two hundred with her. *Athabaskan* rescued thirty-seven of her crew.

Second entry that day: Gallant proceeds to describe the long, slow, journey back to England after the glider-bomb attack. The Tribal and her flotilla brought down four JU88 bombers that day.

> "We had a hard time to get back to port. It took us 5 days, we just made it. We worked night and day along with 19 wounded — one had his two legs blown off, the second night after the action the Germans gave out the news, where they sank a destroyer and left a light cruiser on fire and sinking. The 'destroyer' they sank was [actually] a corvette and the 'cruiser' was us but we managed to stay afloat till we got safely back to port where we all got 21 days leave. The other ships that were with us are all sunk. The *Grenville* was sunk in the Aegean Sea in November 43, the *Orkan* was sunk off the coast of Norway on the 3rd of October 1943, and the other was in the Irish Sea on 2 of December 1943."

After their refit they were out to sea again in December, making a few runs in the Channel and Irish Sea. Then they were sent to the Faroe Islands, and on to North Russia where they patrolled for two days at Kola Bay. On the way to Russia they escorted a large convoy including an aircraft carrier, a couple of cruisers, and a battleship. When they were off Norway an aircraft took off from the carrier and circled the flotilla, including *Athabaskan*, then went straight to the coast where the plane proceeded to sink a large German freighter and a heavy tug. They also shot down a German bomber. Gallant states, "we lost one of our bombers."

On the way back:

> "We left Russia on Xmas Eve where on the way back the *Scharnhorst* was off Bear Island where our battleship and two of our cruisers and a couple of destroyers went after her. We were told to take the convoy through and we were a short way from the *Scharnhorst*. We were in her gun range. We got back safe and on the way our captain told us that the *Scharnhorst* was on fire and sinking soon. He told us that she was sunk and we were mighty glad because we didn't want to have to go to the water in that part of the world for a life wasn't long in the water.
> "On the 26th April, we left our base in Plymouth on a mine laying, escorted a fast minelayer as she laid mines in enemy waters off the coast of France. We fell abreast of the minelayer and we ran at top speed as she laid mines 3 miles from France. After we finished we were on our way back when our RDF picked up enemy ships 50 miles away. We reported it to C-in-C and he sent us a message to investigate. We turned and went

back, us and the *Haida*. We soon caught up and when we were within 1500 yards our captain gave us the order to load, so we did when within 1400 yards, 7 miles on water. Captain gave the order for "B" gun to open fire with Star Shells. "B" gun fired two rounds 4 shells as we waited with excitement to see what kind of ship it was, when the star shells broke we could see quite clear that it was 3 German destroyers.

"We opened fire with "A" and "Y" guns. The Germans fired star shells at us and lit us up like a Xmas tree. We lost no time in firing the second round as the Germans opened fire on us, in our second round we blew the bridge off all the first destroyer and killed 14. We kept firing, the second one laid a smoke screen and there were German shells flying all around us. Some were dropping short and some were going straight over us. Two went through our smoke stack. Finally we caught the third coming out of the smoke screen. We hit her and slowed her down to 20 knots.

"The Captain gave the order 'Salvo Salvo Salvo' which meant to load and fire as fast as we could — for a long while we shelled her. Soon she was all afire and sinking. The captain gave the order to cease firing. We did and we came in close to her so we could see what class destroyer it was. It was *T29*, an Elbing class destroyer with a crew of 228. When we got right close to her she was going down. A machine gun opened on us and near got our crew of "A" gun. I was standing right behind our gun when 2 bullets cut the steel door off of my ready use locker where I was supplying "A" gun. It knocked me back and dazed us for a few seconds — we opened fire and wiped the machine gun's crew out, gun and all, a few minutes later she was out of sight gone under.

"We could see the German sailors in the water but we couldn't stop to pick them up. We found out later that they only had 19 survivors off of her out of a crew of 228. The Germans sent bombers out after us on our way back but the RAF fighter escort came out to meet us and while they engaged the Germans we got back safely in port.

"On the 28 of April we left our base in Plymouth. We were told that we were going to escort a minelayer in laying mines in on the coast of France. We sailed around the Channel until dark and then we ran in on the coast of France. We were in and around the harbour lights of Brest, France. When we were supposed to have finished our job we were told that we were on our way back and we were all quite happy to get out of enemy waters. About 12:03 midnight our RDF picked up enemy ships. We reported it to C-in-C and they told us to investigate, as we did when we got within 1400 yards we fired star shells, then we could see 3 ships and 2 small objects when our star shells broke. The Germans hit us with star shells. We opened fire on them and before we got the second one away there was a great crash, a torpedo got us aft of the ship, which blew the whole of the after part of the ship off including "X" gun and my "Y" gun and only the 4 magazine crews left: charge crew, torpedo crew, sick bay staff and some of the officers' stewards. We kept on firing as our ship was sinking slowly but we didn't fire more than 3 rounds when we got the second torpedo in Number 1 boiler room just one great explosion and everything went in the air, our gun crew — we got underneath the shield of "B" gun to keep from getting hit with burning steel that was coming down — after it quit we got away from there as our ship was sinking fast.

"I just had time to tighten my life belt and kick off my rubber boots and jump over the starboard side as the ship was near on end and falling to port. When I jumped I thought I would never land. When I did and when I came to the top I had no pants on, just my shorts — it was about 4:15 in the morning when we jumped clear of the ship and we were about the last ones to leave. The ship soon went out of sight and all we could hear was the moaning and drowning of some of the crew. The Germans fired star shells over our heads and when they broke I could see most of the swimmers as we used to go up on the swells.

"I found that there were 9 of us together and the rest were a long way from us. Out of the 9, there were 7 of us alive when we got close together. The water was very cold and it would be on the 29 of April. I thought that I would never stand it as they were kicking out one by one. When we got picked up at ten to eight there were 3 of us left and then one fellow died on the deck of the German ship going to Brest, France. I laid on the deck and shivered. I thought that I would never walk again. I was paralyzed from the chest down and it was 2 hours before I could walk. I know that if I had another 5 more minutes I couldn't have stood it. The German said to me for you the war is over and I was mighty glad it was but just didn't know what he meant by it."

Paul recalled that after being taken ashore that first morning and being corralled in a courtyard across from the pier, they witnessed the CAF bombing the town of L'Aber Wrac'h. The bombers flew low over the rooftops and they could feel the vibrations of the destruction three blocks away. The Germans tried desperately to prevent the French people from offering small acts of kindness to the men. The French girls offered the men cigarettes, food, candy and drinks. The new prisoners were taken to a German naval barracks where they were allowed to bathe and change into fresh clothes. Everywhere they looked, the French would make the 'V" sign for victory.

By May 3, 1944, the sailors were boarded onto a train destined for the north of Germany. Paul spent his birthday on that train. The highlights entailed stopping at a water tower to get a drink and being allowed to wash. As they were passing into Germany, the guards pulled the blinds down on the windows trying to discourage the men from witnessing the destruction from the Allied bombing. Food was scarce and the men were starving.

During their time in the POW camp, the men would be witness to numerous air strikes and bombings all around them. On one such occasion, the night of September 7, 1944, in the wee hours of the morning, a "great roar" over the camp awoke the sleeping prisoners from their bunks. A few miles off in the distance, a four-engine bomber had been shot down over a neighbouring village and wiped out three houses and a small brick church as it came down.

Bombings took on a frightening new twist, when for forty-eight days and nights, the skies over Bremen, Hanover and Kiel lit up with the explosion of gunfire and planes falling from the heavens. As though to signal an upcoming attack, the RAF would drop a smoke signal over the camp and the air attacks would begin. The men felt their camp was a marker of sorts for action.

On the 31st of December the camp watched in horror as an air strike high overhead ended with one bomber on fire and the plane plunging to the ground with great speed and eventually crashing in a fiery explosion a hundred yards or so from the camp. As they watched, their mouths agape, four parachutes drifted in the sky, two on fire, narrowly missing the camp.

Another nine parachutists escaped from a fiery plane with one chute failing to open. It was a difficult thing to watch as the airman's arms and legs flailed in the air as he came crashing to the ground a short distance away. In total they witnessed nine planes, both German and RAF destroyed amidst great roars of the mighty engines and clouds of sickening black smoke.

January 1, 1945 brought another round of earth-shattering noise from the sky as a German fighter took off not far from camp, and traveling at breakneck speed, came down over two RAF fighters. Streaks of light could be seen coming from the gunfire from the Allied planes as they repeatedly struck the metal structure of the German planes. That day they witnessed no less than eleven parachutes dropping from the skies.

By February 1, 1945, the Athabaskans were moved to a new camp up the road a half a mile away. They had to move everything themselves; beds, tables, stoves etc. in the pouring rain. Head lice plagued the men, food parcels didn't appear sometimes for six weeks, the camp was overcrowded and the men poorly fed. One day an RAF prisoner across from their camp stopped to speak with one of his guards and a tower guard shot him dead. Conditions were terrible and life was bleak.

On April 5, 1945 Gallant recorded that they ate raw pork with vinegar for supper. The remainder of their feast included bread pudding, cheese, jam, bread, margarine, coffee, sugar, spuds and sardines.

All around them air attacks and gunfire sounded. Once an Allied fighter plane shot up a truck not far from the camp. The pilot flew over the compound, dipped his wings and left. The truck turned out to be their bread truck.

By the end of the first week of April, 1945, the rumble of heavy artillery could be heard throughout the camp as the Allied forces were pushing their way west of Bremen. Fighters continued to clutter the sky and tanks could be heard on the autobahn a mere ten miles away. Standing near their air raid shelter they watched the dog-fighting and the bombing light up the skies with their explosives. In fact, watching the skies became a constant vigil, as the bombers blew up in the air or crashed into fiery rubble on the ground.

Through their treasured radio and the increased activity, they realized liberation was only a short time away. The object of the game was to stay alive long enough in order to enjoy that day.

By April 10, 1945, they were told that all navy men and royal marines were going to be transferred to Lubeck. This entailed a hundred mile march there, while the merchant seamen were to remain behind until the British came. Gallant and five other sailors crawled into a deep hole underneath one of the barracks to avoid going on the march. At the 10:30 a.m. muster, there were only one hundred and fifty-eight out of six hundred inmates. The German officer called in dozens of his guards and rounded up the bloodhounds to sniff out the missing men. However, according to Gallant, the men were one step ahead of the enemy. "We gathered all the pepper we could find and spread it around. It put the hounds off the search."

"The morning was foggy and a lot of fellows cut the wire and got out, some two hundred men." The guards looked under Gallant's barracks and shouted for everyone to come out. The prisoners didn't move, but heard a couple of shots being fired. Eventually the guards moved on to the next barracks. The guards repeated the performance at the next building where some Frenchmen were hiding. Dogs were sent under the building to flush them out. It so happened that two cats, hiding there also, let the dogs know who was boss and sent them running! Only two hundred out of the six hundred prisoners were left to march. "After they left we came out and walked around as bold as could be!" That day, Allied air strikes shot up a truck, killing three of the prisoners, wounding three, and also killing several German guards.

Gallant recorded in his journal that on April 12, 1945 he was walking around the wire of the camp when he witnessed some Russians go by. "There were about twenty-eight or thirty and three guards with them. They were in bad shape. They don't get Red Cross Parcels. Three of them were hauling two that couldn't walk in a wagon. All of us that were standing watching threw cigs, chocolate...matches and everything we could give them. The poor devils were skinning their hands on the wire and when they got down on their knees to pick up the things we gave them, they could hardly get up on their feet again. Each one had a little bag of spuds on their back and their boots wore off their feet."

As the gunfire increased all around them and anticipation of liberation began spiraling upwards, a flag was concocted using a large Red Cross flag and the poles were made ready to hoist their source of pride. By the morning of April 21, 1945 the camp was awakened by the roar of guns at about 2:30 a.m. The bright flashes of a full-blast tank war were going on nearby. Rumours were flying that they were soon to be liberated — either that night or the next morning. The excitement of the camp dwellers spilled out onto the neighbouring inhabitants of a camp housing Poles, Ukrainians, Yugoslavs, Bulgarians and French. After hearing of their imminent freedom, the camp neighbours decided to put on a great feast. "When they were cooking their feed they had a light shining through their windows and a plane spotted them and came down and dropped a bomb and machine gunned their barracks, killing eight and wounding twenty-two. The bomb smashed the window in our barracks and gave us a hell of a fright and cut their barrack right in two. We buried the poor devils in pieces, four to a grave."

The radio reported that Hitler spoke to his people and said he would stay to the last.

Meanwhile the action close to the camp was heating up with massive explosions five miles away in Westertimke. In the distance they witnessed Allied troops burn two neighbouring villages and the women and children from those towns gathered around their camp for safety. Of the initial two hundred camp guards, there were now only a dozen remaining, all over the age of sixty and some in their seventies. The night of April 26, 1945 was spent sleeping in their trench to avoid the shellfire. Gallant notes that "the sound of the explosions were hard on the ears."

By Good Friday, April 30th, 1945, a year to the day of their disaster at sea, the harrowing experience of being held prisoner was quickly coming to a close. On that day the men witnessed the largest air strikes yet as they watched thirteen hundred bombers and seven hundred fighters bomb the surrounding towns of Bremen, Hanover and Cuxhaven Harbour.

The beleaguered Athabaskans gained their freedom and left the camp for the last time in Marlag on May 7, 1945. Gallant had taken ill and had to remain in hospital in Baden before he was air-lifted back to England the following morning. On the designated day of Gallant's return to English soil, he was in the company of one army and one airforce member. Wondering why they were being driven away from the airfield, the servicemen were surprised when the driver of their vehicle swung through the gates to Buckingham Palace. King George had requested that a representative from each of the military services join him for tea. Paul Gallant spent his final day in England enjoying ice cream and tea with King George VI in the gardens of Buckingham Palace. He also pocketed a silver spoon as a memento of his glorious final day; closure to the horrendous ordeal he had endured for the past year.

Paul Gallant's great-granddaughter Nadine Howick-Griffin was to serve on HMCS *Athabaskan* III six decades later.

James Alexander Vair
A-4980
Leading Steward
October 18, 1913 – April 29, 1944

Some Athabaskans were already enjoying married life at home in Canada when they were called to enlist. It was a great sacrifice to leave your loved ones behind for months and years on end while off to battle. This was especially true of young twenty-nine-year-old Jim Vair from Northern Ontario. He left behind his wife Norma and two small children, a ten-month-old son William, and a two-year-old daughter, Norma Jean.

Vair wrote his beloved wife as frequently as possible. One can only imagine how much letters were anticipated on both sides of the Atlantic. He affectionately nicknamed his wife Sally, and Norma Jean became Sally Ann. The following are excerpts of his letters home to his precious family. There can be nothing more heart-wrenching than the poignancy of letters to your little girl on the outside chance you won't return from war.

> "Hello me daughter:
> It will be quite some time before you will be able to read these lines. But when the time comes as you grow older, I as your father, sincerely hope they may bring you a little pleasure, a little comfort; possibly in time of doubt they may contain something that will help you. And if they accomplish any of these, why then it will have doubled the pleasure it gives me in writing to you."

As Vair proceeds with his fatherly advice, he says:

> "In this game that I am a very insignificant member of, anything can happen. We all hope for the best and to be together after it is finished. But in case anything occurs, I would like you to have a few lines from your 'Daddy Jim.'"

Vair was very touched by an officer who spoke of his own father's philosophy on life. He writes to Sally Ann recalling the officer's words of wisdom:

> "If you can do a hundred good turns, do them and if one is repaid or thanks given in kind, then you are doubly paid for them all. If it is in your power to lend a helping hand, do so without thought of reward. You will find that the inner glow of 'conscience' having done a good deed voluntarily, will give you a feeling that nothing on earth can replace. It is the little things in life that give you the most pleasure.
>
> "A small cup of water to a working man is worth more than a pail of gold dust. Have a kindly thought for all folk. Never judge by a surface look. But reserve an opinion for deeper study."

In May of 1942 he writes Sally Ann:

> "Life is like a hill. Walk up it straight and you enjoy the view from the top. Stop and wander down the byways on the way up, and the top has yet to be reached. Walk up Life straight."

In the Mess one night he sat down to write his letters home to Sally Ann once again. He wanted to give his daughter a visual image so she could imprint it in her memory in case anything should happen to him.

> "Daughter, as I sit in our Mess writing to you I am dressed in me blue trousers, heavy boots, shirt of white, opened at the throat, a black sweater knitted for me by your Mother in the early days of our marriage, with me pipe going half the time, the other half I'm lighting it.
>
> "The sweater is black, sweater coat in fact, with a zipper front, the cuffs are turned up about two inches on the right side, one on the left.
>
> "I tell you this, for I imagine you will try to picture me as these words are written and ten chances to one, that is exactly as I shall be dressed each time I pen words to you."

As a father, Vair ponders over the insightful life's lessons he wishes to leave his dear Sally Ann, in the event that war should claim him as a casualty.

> "Everything in life grows up. Trees grow up toward the heavens, flowers grow up towards the sun, babies grow into men and women and, if they walk life straight, they grow to God, our Creator and our Friend and when our span of life is over, they go up to heaven. —Daddy Jim."

Vair was below deck on April 29, 1944. It was inevitable he was unable to make it top-side after the explosion, and perished on the ship. He is officially classified as "Missing Presumed Dead." His body was never recovered.

APPENDIX A

Company On *Athabaskan*'s Final Patrol April 28/29, 1944

List reproduced from *Unlucky Lady: the Life and Death of HMCS* Athabaskan,
L. Burrows and E. Beaudoin, courtesy of McClelland & Stewart.

Name	Number	Rank	Age	Domicile	Fate
1. ACORN, John J.	V-1589	L.Sto.	20	Cardigan, PEI	POW
2. ADAMS, John C.	V-17001	AB	31	London, ON	MPD
3. AGNEW, John	V-1383	AB	22	Charlottetown, PEI	MPD
4. AIKINS, James O.	V-64833	OS	19	Toronto, ON	Haida
5. ALLISON, Albert E.	V-8402	AB	30	Hamilton, ON	MPD
6. AMIRO, Irvin V.	V-26054	Tel	21	Pubnico.NS	Plouescat
7. ANNETT, Robert I.L.	0-2450	Sub.Lieut.(E)	19	Consort, AB	Plouescat
8. ARMSTRONG, George	V-12833	AB	24	Frt.Saskatchewan	Plouescat
9. ASHTON, PERCY G.	V-31508	AB	19	Toronto, ON	MPD
10. AUDET, Jean F.A.	V-35565	AB	21	Montreal, PQ	Haida(C)
11. BACKUS, Robert G.	V-12122	PO	32	Victoria, BC	Haida
12. BANKDICK, Paul V.	V-53713	OS	22	Brandon, MB	Haida
13. BARRETT, Arthur E.	V-12346	AB	26	Edmonton, AB	Plouescat
14. BARTON, John J.	V-32345	ERA (4)	24	Sudbury, On	Haida
15. BEACH, Ernest R.	V-10831	AB	24	Balgonie, SK	POW
16. BEAUDOIN, Arthur E.	V-3690	L.Tel.	24	Quebec, PQ	POW
17. BELL, Donald A.	V-53224	Sto. (1)	20	London, ON	Plouescat
18. BELL, Joseph A.	4339	AB	21	Victoria, BC	POW
19. BENNETTS, Henry, J.	3271	L.Tel	24	Esquimalt, BC	Haida
20. BERKELEY, Alfred G.	V-54498	OS	19	Edmonton, AB	MPD
21. BERTRAND, Laurent J.	2408	CPO	33	Halifax, N.S.	Plouescat
22. BIANCO, Anthony D.	V34263	AB	19	Peterborough, ON	MPD
23. BIEBER, Edgar E.	V-9844	Sto.PO	27	Winnipeg, MB	MPD
24. BINT, Benjamin W.	V-11479	AB	21	Saskatoon, SK	POW
25. BLINCH, Harry C.	4265	AB	21	Abbotsford, BC	MPD
26. BOWER, Milton C.	A-4553	AB	26	Jordan Falls, NS	POW
27. BRANDSON, Thomas	0-8360	Pay-Lieut	28	Winnipeg, MB	MPD
28. BRIGHTEN, Victor	21930	ERA (2)	25	Verdun PQ	MPD
29. BUCK. Stanley J.	V-27655	AB	21	Toronto, ON	Haida(C)
30. BURGESS, Arthur	V-31538	AB	22	Prince Albert, SK	POW
31. BURGESS, Charles	2438	CPO	31	Victoria, BC	Haida (C)

32. BURROW, Wm.O.	V-7988	LS	22	Toronto, ON	MPD
33. BURROWS, Berchman	V-32266	LS	21	Ottawa, ON	POW
34. BUSHIE, Victor A.	V-22240	LS	24	Halifax, NS	Haida
35. CAMPBELL, George M.	V-56444	AB	32	New Waterford NS	POW
36. CARR, John J.	V-9472	AB	28	Winnipeg, MB	Haida
37. CASWELL, George	V-7823	PO	24	Victoria, BC	Haida(C)
38. CATTANI, Robert	V-16567	LS	21	Port Arthur, ON	Haida
39. CHADSEY, Allen	4174	L.Sgm	21	Vancouver, BC	Haida
40. CHAMBERLAND, Paul	V-3677	AB	22	Quebec, PQ	Plougasnou
41. CLARK, Wm.	0-14130	Lieut.	29	Montreal, PQ	POW
42. CLARKE, Stanley	V23104	AB	25	Verdun, PQ	POW
43. CONNOLLY, Wm.E.	V-40271	Sgm	23	Hamilton, ON	POW
44. COOKMAN, Edgar	3210	LS	23	Esquimalt, BC	MPD
45. COONEY, Stewart	V-35579	Stwd.	21	Belleville, ON	MPD
46. COOPER, Hector	40532	SY CPO	26	Head of Jeddore, NS	POW
47. CORBIERE, Vincent	V-34003	AB	20	St. Catharines, ON	MPD
48. CORKUM, Gordon	A-1169	AB	24	Halifax, NS	Pornic
49. COTTRELL, Sydney	V-18362	AB	23	Trenton, ON	Plouescat
50. COWLEY, Arthur	V-41591	AB	37	Oshawa, ON	POW
51. CROFT, Moyle H.	A-4958	AB	31	Rose Bay, NS	MPD
52. CROSS, Alfred	V-25039	O.Tel	26	Armdale, NS	MPD
53. CUMMINS, Ralph	V-11692	L.Sto.	22	Wild Rose, SK	POW
54. DALZELL, Robert	4141	AB	23	Prescott, ON	POW
55. DEAL, Cornelius	V-31445	AB	26	S. Rawdon, NS	POW
56. DeARMOND, Gordon	V-11568	LS	22	Saskatoon, SK.	MPD
57. DEMPSEY, Frank	V-59818	OS	20	Toronto, ON	POW
58. DEMPSEY, Wm.	C-33968	Tel.	29	Winnipegosis, MB	Haida
59. DICK, Stanley	V-7995	LS	22	Toronto, ON	POW
60. DILLEN, Stewart	V-34261	Stwd.	27	Brockville, ON	MPD
61. DION, Albert	V-3373	L.Sto	24	Quebec, PQ	MPD
62. DOLAN, John	V-35529	Sto. (1)	21	Batley, Yorkshire	POW
63. DOWNEY, John	V-23421	Sgm.	23	Montreal, PQ	POW
64. DUNNELL, Stephen	V-30419	Or.Art (2)	37	Victoria, BC	POW
65. EADY, Thomas	V-19177	Sgm.	24	Welland, ON	Haida(C)
66. EDHOUSE, Donald	V-58286	Sto.(2)	23	Toronto, ON	MPD
67. EDWARDS, John	V-12916	AB	24	Edmonton, AB	Haida
68. EDWARDS, Lloyd	V-16555	AB	20	Fort William, ON	POW
69. EVANS, James	2390	CPO	37	Halifax, NS	POW
70. FAIRCHILD, John	V-4709	AB	19	Quebec, PQ	POW
71. FILLATRE, Samuel	A-5043	AB	25	Purcell's Cove, NS	POW
72. FLEMING, Harold	V-12849	AB	28	Calgary, AB	MPD

73. FORRON, Jack	V-17506	Sto.(1)	20	London, ON	MPD
74. FRALICK, Earl	V-31885	AB	22	Port Dufferin, NS	MPS
75. FREES, Wm.	A-2712	Sto.PO	27	Dalhousie Juncion, NB	POW
76. FRITH, Wm.	V-17806	LS	20	London, ON	Plouescat
77. FULLER, Eugene	V-8808	AB	24	Brantford, ON	Plouescat
78. FYFE, James	0-25690	Surg.Lieut	30	Winnipeg, MB	POW
79. GAETANO, Valentino	V-35858	AB	20	Sault Ste. Marie, ON	MPD
80. GALLANT, Paul	A-1889	AB	29	Tignish, PEI	POW
81. GIBBONS, Marshall	V-51109	AB	19	London, ON	Brignogan-Plages
82. GOLDSMITH, Thomas	2980	CYS	27	Victoria, BC	Plouescat
83. GORDON, Lloyd	V-1267	AB	23	Clyde River, NS	MPD
84. GOULET, Antoine	V-42224	Sto (1)	21	Ottawa, ON	POW
85. GOULET, Robert	V-42673	Sto (1)	20	Ottawa, ON	MPD
86. GRACIE, Robert	V-36493	Sto (1)	23	Toronto, ON	Haida
87. GRAINGER, Roy	V-17877	LSA	27	Port Hope, ON	MPD
88. GRENIER, Roger	V-33249	AB	20	Verdun, PQ	POW
89. GUEST, Carlton	V-17487	AB	20	London, ON	Plouescat
90. HAYES, Christopher	V-34725	OS	28	Toronto, ON	MPD
91. HAYES, Wm.	V-8722	L.Coder	30	Hamilton, ON	Haida
92. HAYWARD, Robin	0-31940	Lieut.	23	Duncan, BC	POW
93. HEARL, John	V-69248	AB	22	New Westminster, BC	POW
94. HEATHERINGTON, John	V-31647	Sto(1)	21	Regina, SK	MPD
95. HENRICKSON, Wilfred	V-16590	AB	20	Allanwater, ON	POW
96. HENRY, Robert	V-16777	AB	20	Fort William, ON	Ile de Batz
97. HESLER, Geoffrey	V-23323	Cook (S)	21	Montreal, PQ	POW
98. HESTON, P.	C/MX678680	Wrtr (SP)	24	London, England	MPD
99. HEWITT, Ted	V-17860	AB	22	Woodstock, ON	Haida
100. HINDS, Edward	V-6477	ERA	24	Timmons, ON	Haida
101. HOLWELL, John	V-8875	AB	20	Hamilton, ON	POW
102. HOPKINS, Robert	V-35886	Sto(1)	19	Sherbrooke, PQ	POW
103. HOUISON, George	V-23114	L.Wrtr.	24	Hamilton, ON	MPD
104. HOWARD, George	V-1468	AB	25	Kensington, PEI	POW
105. HOWARD, Wm	V-40160	ERA(5)	20	Niagara Falls, ON	Haida
106. Hubbard, Frederick	V-44405	Sto.PO	30	St. Catharines, On	POW
107. HURLEY, Michael	V-36734	Sto(1)	30	Toronto, ON	MPD
108. HURWITZ, Harry	V-31067	AB	22	Montreal, PQ	POW
109. IRVINE, Leonard	V-11886	AB	20	Saskatoon, SK	Plouescat
110. IZARD, Theodore	0-35880	Lieut (E)	26	Victoria, BC	MPD
111. JAKO, Leonard	21818	L.Sto.	24	Vancouver, BC	Haida
112. JARVIS, Edmund	3330	LS	23	Morrisburg, ON	MPD
113. JOHNSON, Elswood	V-16839	AB	19	Edmonton, AB	MPD

114. JOHNSON, Ira	2792	CPO	25	Saint John, NB	POW
115. JOHNSON, Richard	V-5801	L.Sto.	23	Hamilton, ON	MPD
116. JOHNSTON, Lawrence	V-51370	AB	19	Winnipeg, MB	Plouescat
117. KANE, John	V-8971	LS	24	Hamilton, ON	Haida
118. KELLY, James	3670	PO	24	Calgary, AB	POW
119. KELLY, Lionel	V-4445	Stwd.	24	Montreal, PQ	MPD
120. KETTLES, Stuart	V-6748	L.Wrtr.	26	Ottawa, ON	POW
121. KING, John	V-48770	AB	19	Saint John, NB	POW
122. KNIGHT, Russell	3209	PO	24	Grand Pairie, AB	Haida
123. KOBES, John	3074	LS	24	Victoria, BC	MPD
124. LAIDLER, John	V-11667	AB	24	Saskatoon, SK	POW
125. LAMBERT, Wm.	V-5883	Tel	24	Montreal, PQ	Haida
126. LAMOUREUX, Andre	V-4348	LS	22	Montreal, PQ	POW
127. LANTIER, Dunn	0-40520	Lieut-Com	27	Montreal, PQ	POW
128. LAURIE, Douglas	21532	Sto.PO	25	Port Alberni, BC	POW
129. LAURIN Bernard	40748	L.Cook (S)	24	Perkinsfield, ON	Haida
130. LAWRENCE, Ralph	0-40930	Lieut	24	Glasgow, Scotland	MPD
131. LEA, Eric	V-47397	Sto (1)	21	Victoria, BC	MPD
132. LEDOUX, Louis	V-4433	AB	21	Montreal, PQ	Plouescat
133. LEGGETT, Reginald	V-33303	L.Sto	26	Worthing, Sussex	POW
134. LEGH, Norris	V-36139	L.Coder	25	New Westminster, BC	Haida
135. L'ESPERANCE, Joseph	V-9580	LS	26	Winnipeg, MB	POW
136. LEWANDOWSKI, Stanley	V-61813	Sto (2)	19	Windsor, On	MPD
137. LIND, Mekkel	V-13918	Sto.PO	28	Innisfail, AB	MPD
138. LIZNICK, Harry	V-33930	AB	20	Montrock, ON	POW
139. LOVE, Alexander	V-8620	C.Sto	24	Welland, ON	Haida
140. LOVE, Walter	V-8030	ERA(3)	40	Dartmouth NS	MPD
141. LUCAS, Donald	V-60018	Sto (2)	19	Winnipeg, MB	MPD
142. LYNCH, Donald	V-13359	PO Tel.	23	Calgary, AB	Haida
143. MacAVOY, Gerald	40500	PO Cook (0)	27	Halifax, NS	MPD
144. MacDONALD, Ashley	3625	AB	23	Ottawa, ON	MPD
145. MacDONALD, Hugh	V-58962	Sto (2)	19	Toronto, ON	Haida
146. MacKENZIE, Alexander	V-19875	AB	22	Riverside, ON	MPD
147. MacNEILL, Glenn	V-49124	OS	20	Regina, SK	POW
148. MAGUIRE, John	40911	L.Sto	25	Evansburg, AB	Plouescat
149. MAHONEY, John	0-45890	Lieut (SP)	22	Toronto, ON	Plouescat
150. MANCOR, Claude	40464	Sto.PO	25	Irma, AB	Haida
151. MANSON, John	V-23559	Cook (0)	26	Montreal, PQ	Plouescat
152. MARTIN, James	V-44560	Tel.	19	Westmount, PQ	POW
153. MARTIN, Wm.	V-45798	Tel	23	Hamilton, ON	Haida
154. MATTHEWS, George	V-2809	AB	22	Red Head, NB	MPD

155. McBRIDE, John	V-45461	AB	19	Winnipeg, MB	Plouescat
156. McCABE, Jese	V-34420	AB	23	Prince George, BC	POW
157. McCARROLL, Thomas	V-39522	Sto (1)	22	Hamilton, ON	MPD
158. McCLOY, Edward	V-18488	AB	23	Brockville, ON	POW
159. McCRINDLE, Wm	V-1854	AB	23	Nipawin, SK	MPD
160. McGREGOR, Wm	V-30291	L.Sto.	32	Victoria, BC	Plouescat
161. McKEEMAN, Lester	A-4311	AB	34	Gaspereaux, PEI	POW
162. McLEAN, Daniel	V-14742	AB	23	Vancouver, BC	MPD
163. McNEIL, John	V-59518	Sto(2)	20	New Victoria, BC	Landeda
164. MEADWELL, Richard	V-49203	AB	20	Sioux Lookout, ON	MPD
165. MELOCHE, Raymond	V-35940	AB	20	Montreal, PQ	POW
166. MENGONI, Eric	3980	AB	23	Dartmouth, NS	MPD
167. METCALFE, Donald	V-11603	El.Art (3)	32	Vancouver, BC	MPD
168. MILLAR, Victor	V-27555	AB	28	Lakeview, ON	MPD
169. MILLER, Joseph	V-3922	OS	24	Quebec, PQ	Haida
170. MILLS, Ernest	21508	C.ERA	27	Saanich, BC	MPD
171. MITCHELL, Wm	A-3042	C.Sto.	42	Vancouver, BC	POW
172. MOAR, Raymond	V-34808	AB	27	Chatham, NB	POW
173. MUMFORD, Leonard	V-42353	ERA (4)	25	Hagersville, ON	MPD
174. MYETTE, Vincent	A-5095	AB	25	Tracadie, NS	POW
175. NASH, Robert	O-54790	Sub.Lieut	22	Seattle, Washington	Plouescat
176. NEAVES, Harry	40844	El.Art (3)	28	Victoria, BC	Haida
177. NEWLOVE, Thomas	V-11936	Cook (S)	22	Star City, SK	Haida
178. NEWMAN, Donald	V-31264	AB	19	Calgary, AB	POW
179. NICHOLAS, Joseph	V-16615	L.Sto.	22	Fort William, ON	MPD
180. NORRIS, Guy	V-48316	Sgm.	24	Nelson, BC	Haida(C)
181. O'BRIEN, Earl	V-26333	Sto.PO	24	New Waterford, NS	Haida
182. OGILVIE, Robert	V-27800	SBPO	24	London, ON	POW
183. OSBORNE, Robert	V-11851	AB	20	Saskatoon, SK	POW
184. OUELLETTE, Joseph	V-50769	AB	20	Sabreoix, PQ	MPD
185. PARSONS, George	V-18056	AB	26	Belleville, ON	Haida
186. PARSONS, Gordon	V-25782	L.Sto.	25	North Sydney, NS	POW
187. PEART, Hubert	A-927	AB	28	Glace Bay NS	MPD
188. PHILLIPS, John	V-19152	AB	24	Windsor, ON	Plouescat
189. PHILLIPS, Russell	V-926	AB	22	Ocean Falls, BC	POW
190. PIKE, Brenton	V-36417	AB	22	Saint John, NB	Plouescat
191. POLSON, Edwin	V-33438	Sto.(1)	29	Ville La Salle, PQ	POW
192. POTHIER, Charles	V-4752	AB	19	Yarmouth, NS	Brest
193. QUIGLEY, George	V-7980	L.Tel.	24	Toronto, ON	Haida
194. RENNIE, John	3075	PO	23	Kelowna, BC	MPD
195. RICHARDSON, Alfred	A-5468	L.Cook(S)	25	West Dover, NS	Haida

196. RIENDEAU, Joseph	V-6869	AB	21	Ottawa, ON	Plouescat
197. ROBERTS, John	V-41049	ERA(4)	22	Stratford, ON	MPD
198. ROBERTS, Raymond	V-10880	AB	22	Moose Jaw, SK	Plouescat
199. ROBERTSHAW, Eric	V-8634	AB	21	Hamilton, ON	Plouescat
200. ROBERTSON, Ian	V-33909	AB	20	Saskatoon, SK	Plouescat
201. ROBERTSON, Wm.	V-55418	Sto.(1)	37	Glasgow, Scotland	MPD
202. ROCK, J.M.G.	C/MX677366	Wrtr(SP)	24	London, England	Haida
203. ROGER, Leo	V-38436	Sto.(1)	22	Toronto, ON	Plouescat
204. ROLLS, Raymond	V-34863	AB	21	St. Stephen, NB	Plouescat
205. ROUSE, Edward	V-37897	Sto.(1)	21	Tillsonburg, ON	POW
206. RUTHERFORD, Norman	PMX-124283	Rad.Mech PO	24	London, England	MPD
207. RYAN, Norman V.	V-52603	AB	19	Sault Ste. Marie, ON	MPD
208. ST. LAURENT, Joseph	V-37192	AB	20	Quebec, PQ	MPD
209. SAMPSON, Francis	V-174	AB	27	Halifax, NS	Plouescat
210. SANDERSON, Earl	V-34973	AB	24	Midgell, PEI	MPD
211. SAUNDERS, Walter	V-2801	AB	22	Saint John, NB	POW
212. SAVAGE, Francis	4761	LS	23	Edmonton, AB	Haida
213. SCANLON, Delbert	V-7702	Sgm.	26	Toronto, ON	POW
214. SCOTT, John	0-65660	Lieut.	22	Halifax, NS	Haida
215. SCRATCH, Elmer	V-50726	AB	20	Blytheswood, ON	POW
216. SENECAL, Jean	V-15272	AB	20	St.Vincent de Paul, PQ	Plouescat
217. SHARP, Kenneth	4316	AB	24	Toronto, ON	Haida
218. SHEA, John	21801	C.ERA	24	Winnipeg, MB	Haida
219. SHEPPARD, Walter	4420	Tel.	20	Vancouver, BC	POW
220. SHERLOCK, Albert	V-861	Stwd.	33	St. Lambert, PQ	MPD
221. SIGSTON, George	0-66930	Gun.	32	Dartmouth, NS	MPD
222. SIMALUK, Walter	V-10998	AB	24	Regina, SK	POW
223. SINGLETON, John	V-17334	AB	29	Delaware, ON	MPD
224. SKYVINGTON, Francis	V-46829	SBA	19	Toronto, ON	MPD
225. SMYTH, James	V-6532	AB	33	Ottawa, ON	POW
226. SOMMERFELD, Samuel	V-32952	AB	20	Saskatoon, SK	MPD
227. SOUCISSE, Paul	V-836	Coder	23	Montreal, PQ	MPD
228. STATZ, Clarence	V-46767	OS	22	Edmonton, AB	POW
229. STENNING, Raymond	40848	CPO Cook (S)	26	Victoria, BC	POW
230. STEVENSON, Elmer	V-53221	Sto.(1)	23	Havelock, ON	MPD
231. STEVENSON, Richard	0-69990	Lieut.	24	Montreal, PQ	POW
232. STEWART, John	V-1362	AB	32	Charlottetown, PEI	MPD
233. STEWART, Wm.	V-8866	Sgm	22	Hamilton, ON	MPD
234. STOCKMAN, Ernest	0-70390	Lieut.(E)	35	Toronto, ON	MPD
235. STUBBS, John	0-70990	Lieut.-Com	31	Victoria, BC	Plouescat
236. SULKERS, Herm	V-24660	AB	23	East Kildonan, MB	POW

237. SUTHERLAND, John	V-12533	AB	21	Edmonton, AB	MPD
238. SUTHERLAND, Wm.	V-36523	Sto.(1)	19	Winnipeg, MB	POW
239. SWEENEY, Daniel	V-23913	AB	20	Montreal, PQ	POW
240. SWEET, Charles	2563	CPO	30	Victoria, BC	Plouescat
241. TAKALO, Ernest	V-33953	Sto(1)	19	Port Arthur, ON	Haida
242. THERIAULT, Joseph	V-38688	Sto(1)	21	Montreal, PQ	Haida
243. THOMPSON, Harry	V-38485	Sto(1)	20	Montreal, PQ	MPD
244. THRASHER, Allen	3654	L.Sgm	22	Toronto, ON	POW
245. TOURANGEAU, Joseph	V-3650	AB	22	Quebec, PQ	POW
246. TRICKETT, Wm.	V-38773	AB	20	Kelwood, MB	POW
247. TUPPER, Allister	V-40751	Or.Art(4)	26	New Glasgow, NS	MPD
248. TYRIE, James	V-18295	Cook(S)	21	Kingston, ON	POW
249. VAIR, James	A-4980	L.Stwd	30	St. Joseph's Is., ON	MPD
250. VEINOTTE, Joseph	V-25606	Sy PO	27	Marie Joseph, NS	MPD
251. WAITSON, Maurice	V-18646	AB	19	Napanee, ON	MPD
252. WALLACE, Peter	V-11722	AB	21	Saskatoon, SK	MPD
253. WARD, Leslie	0-76040	Lieut.(SB)	36	Ottawa, ON	MPD
254. WATSON, Reginald	V-35953	Tel.	23	New York, NY	Plouescat
255. WEBSTER, Gerald	V-11468	LS	24	Saskatoon, SK	POW
256. WESTAWAY, Roy	V-34915	AB	19	Toronto, ON	POW
257. WILLIAMS, Kenneth	A-5402	ERA(4)	33	Peterborough, ON	Plouescat
258. WILLOCK, Samuel	V-52873	SA	37	Vancouver, BC	POW
259. WOOD, John	V-34862	AB	28	Hampstead, NB	Pornic
260. YEADON, Robert	V-272	AB	23	Halifax, NS	Ile de Batz
261. YOUNG, Charles	V-41759	Shipwrt.(4)	42	London, ON	Haida
262. GINGER (SHIP'S CAT)	GO7	Mascot	2	Newcastle, England	MPD

Legend for Column Six

Brest	Buried in Kerfautras Cemetary, Brest, Finistere, France
Brignogan-Plages	Buried at Brignogan-Plages, Finistere, France
Ile de Batz	Buried on Ile de Batz, Finistere, France
Haida	Rescued by HMCS Haida
Haida (C)	Rescued by Haida's Cutter
Landeda	Buried at Landeda, Finistere, France
MPD	Missing Presumed Dead
Plouescat	Buried at Plouescat, Finistere, France
Plougasnou	Buried at Plougasnow, Finistere, France
Pornic	Buried at Pornic, Loire-Inferieure, France
POW	Prisoner of War

Two unidentified Athabaskan sailors lie in the cemetery of Sibiril, France, and another unidentified Athabaskan sailor lies in the French cemetery of Cleden Cap Sizun.

APPENDIX B
Glossary

AFT: At or towards the stern of a ship.

BEAM: Term used for the width of a vessel.

CARLEY FLOAT: Lifesaving device with slat floor suspended inside a floating tube. Paddles are provided the twenty-foot long, five-foot wide float will support twelve people inside and eight clinging to the lifeline attached to the outer edge.

DOCKYARD MATEYS: Dockyard workmen, who assisted in ship construction and repairs.

ELBING: According to Wikipedia. The Elbing class torpedo boats (or Flottentorpedoboot 1939) Were a class of fifteen small warships that served in the Kriegsmarine in World War II. They were comparabe to contemporary British medium-size destroyers.

U-BOAT: Small, highly maneuverable German motor torpedo boats.

POM POM: Single or multi-barrelled automatic gun firing a two-pound shell.

PORT SIDE: Looking forward, the left side of a ship.

RATING: ny non-commissioned sailor.

SCRAMBLE NET: Weighted nets made of cordage used to allow people floating in the water alongside a rescuing ship to climb up her side.

STARBOARD SIDE: Looking forward, the right side of a ship.

APPENDIX C
List of Sources

PART ONE

Chapters One and Two:

    Personal interviews with Noreen Baker, Anthony Holmes and Ralph Mellow.

Chapter Three:

    Personal and telephone interviews with Ralph Mellow and Anthony Holmes.

    Personal Interviews with Herm Sulkers, April 29, 2001 and May, 2002.

    Service Records, National Archives of Canada.

Chapter Four:

    Unlucky Lady: The Life and Death of HMCS Athabaskan 1940-1944, Len Burrows and Emile Beaudoin, Canada's Wings Inc, 1982.

    Service Records for Maurice Waitson.

Chapters Five, Six and Seven:

    Unlucky Lady, Burrows and Beaudoin.

    HMCS Haida: *Battle Ensign Flying*, Barry M. Gough, St. Catharines: Vanwell Publishing Ltd., 2001.

    The Canadians At War 1939-1945, Second Edition, The Reader's Digest Association Ltd. 1986.

    Canada's Navy: The First Century, Marc Milner, Toronto: University of Toronto Press, 1999.

    The Unlucky Lady, documentary, National Film Board, 1984.

    Unlucky Lady: The Life and Death of HMCS Athabaskan, documentary, Northern Sky Entertainment, 2001.

    The Mysterious Sinking of HMCS Athabaskan, documentary, Northern Sky Entertainment, 2004

    The Montreal Gazette, September 2, 1980

    "Battle of the Atlantic", *Trident*, April 20, 2009

    "Athabaskan Missing", *The Globe and Mail*, May 5, 1944

    Personal Interviews with: Herm Sulkers, John Fairchild, Glen MacNeill, William Connolly, Ralph Frayne, Wilf Henrickson, Harry Hurwitz, and John Ulhmann.

    Wayne Abbott, personal correspondence

    Michael Whitby personal correspondence

    Letter from Moe to Ralph, courtesy of Ralph Mellow, property of author.

    Letter from Moe to Noreen Baker, property of author.

Chapters Eight, Nine and Ten:

    Personal Stories of author.

    Personal Interviews with Noreen Baker, Herm Sulkers, and John Fairchild.

Chapters Eleven, Twelve and Thirteen:

    Personal Experience.

    Interviews with: Herm Sulkers, Wilf Henrickson, Jacques Ouchakoff, M. and Mme. Elie Boisson.

PART TWO

    Lt.Cdr. John H. Stubbs: *Unlucky Lady*, Burrow and Beaudoin.

    Herman Sulkers: Personal Interviews 2001- 2006. Correspondence with Neil Sulkers.

    William Connolly: Personal Interviews with William and Vi Connolly.

    Vi Connolly: Personal Interviews with Vi Connolly.

    John Fairchild: Personal Interviews with John and Pam Fairchild, 2001 - 2009.

Simon Muzyka: Personal correspondence, September 2009.

Sydney Cottrell: Information provided by Douglas Cottrell.

Ralph Frayne: Personal correspondence, August to October 2009.

Glenn MacNeill: Personal correspondence, February to October of 2009.

Lt. Jack Scott: Information provided by Dr. Caroline Scott.

Wilfred Henrickson: Personal correspondence and interviews, July 2003 to April, 2009.

George (Buck) Parsons: Information provided by Ardel Hitchon.

Lt. Robin Hayward: Information provided by Sarah Hayward.

John Uhlmann: Personal interview, June 26 2009.

Ernest Takalo: Written account provided by Ernest Takalo, January 2009.

Ted Hewitt: Information provided courtesy of Kim Hewitt.

Leslie Ward: Information provided courtesy of Peter Ward.

Stuart Kettles: Information provided courtesy of Bruce Kettles.

Robert Dalzell: Information obtained from personal war diary, courtesy of Ron and Joan Reynolds.

William Stewart: Information provided courtesy of Edward and Hugh Stewart.

Harry Hurwitz: Personal Interview, January 2009, and war diary courtesy of Harry Hurwitz.

Samuel Fillatre: Information obtained from war diary, letters, and memorabilia, courtesy of Jean Fillatre, January 2009.

Ingar Laurie: Telephone interview, May 2009. Additional information provided courtesy of Gayle Buie.

Douglas Laurie: Information provided by Ingar Laurie and Gayle Buie.

Andre Audet: Friends of the Canadian War Museum Oral History Project, CVM20020121 -004, George Metcalf Archival Collection, Canadian War Museum.

Joseph L'Esperance: Information provided by Jim L'Esperance and Sharon Schinke.

Paul Gallant: Information obtained from war diary, courtesy of Max Gallant and Nadine Howick-Giffin.

James Vair: Letters and information provided by William Vair.

Company on Athabaskan's Final Patrol – courtesy of McClelland & Stewart.

"Channel Patrol" painted and donated as a memorial to Fort Montbarey, Brest, France by Sherry Pringle.

Plaque reads: "The Canadian Destroyer HMCS Athabaskan was sunk in combat on April 29, 1944 near Ile de Vierge. Dedicated to the memory of the 261 sailors of whom 128 perished participating in the liberation of France and in homage to the Bretons who perpetually remember their sacrifice.

      "And life is eternal and love is immortal,

       and death is only a horizon,

       and a horizon is nothing save

        the limit of our sight."

         St. Bede

ABOUT THE AUTHOR
Sherry J. Pringle

An accomplished artist, Sherry lives with her husband Larry and their westie, Maddy, along the quiet shores of the Napanee River, just a short distance downstream from her Uncle Moe's favourite fishing haunt. Her studio overlooks the river where her story begins, and if you follow its route, you will discover that it ends with her story, in France.